The Learner's Path

Practices for Recovering Knowers

Brian Hinken

Pegasus Communications, Inc.
Waltham, Massachusetts

PEGASUS COMMUNICATIONS, INC.
One Moody Street
Waltham, MA 02453-5339 USA
Phone 800-272-0945 / 781-398-9700
Fax 781-894-7175
customerservice@pegasuscom.com info@pegasuscom.com

www.pegasuscom.com

Library of Congress Cataloging-in-Publication Data

Hinken, Brian.
The learner's path : practices for recovering knowers / Brian Hinken.--
1st ed.
p. cm.
Includes bibliographical references.
ISBN 1-883823-10-2 (978-1-883823-10-8)
1. Adult learning. 2. Self-actualization (Psychology) 3. self culture.
I. Title.
LC5225.L42H56 2007
370.15'23--dc22
2007035545

Source Credits:

p. 15 Permission to reprint the photo has been granted from *Water Ski & Wakeboard Canada*.

p. 38–39 Permission to reprint "Fights, weather, reduce island's gray wolf population" (March 8, 2002, 6B) has been granted by the *Muskegon Chronicle*.

p. 42–43 Reprinted by permission of Harvard Business School Publishing. From "Tool: Assessing Your Workplace Mental Models" in *Managing Difficult Conversations* (supplementary material) by Bill Noonan, Chris Argyris, and Peter M. Senge. Copyright © 2007 by the Harvard Business School Publishing Corporation; all rights reserved.

Acquiring and Project Editor: Janice Molloy
Production and Revised Design: Nancy Daugherty
Original Design: Boynton Hue Studio

Printed on recycled paper
Printed and bound in Canada
First edition
First printing September 2007

5793

12 11 10 09 08 07 10 9 8 7 6 5 4 3 2 1

For Faith

who, above all others, helps me live as a learner.

Contents

Acknowledgments

FOR THOSE WHOSE SHOULDERS I STAND UPON

The Learner's Path stands in the shadow of the works of many outstanding practitioners of organizational learning who have come before me. My first acknowledgment must be to Peter Senge for articulating in *The Fifth Discipline*, and then later with his colleagues in *The Fifth Discipline Fieldbook*, a way to be more effective in the world. My material wraps itself around, and stands on the foundation of, Peter's original and influential works.

The first serious academic studying I did after graduate school has centered on the works of Chris Argyris. He has been like a virtual mentor for me, and his ideas have been a fulcrum on which I balance my understanding of learning. The works of Chris Argyris and Peter Senge sit on my shelf, next to my Bible, in my most prized location.

Fred Kofman's writing has stimulated my thinking about knowers and learners more than any other author. Way before these concepts coalesced in my mind, I was mailing my dollars to Colorado in exchange for his printed articles, which I subsequently collected in a 3-ring binder and referred to through the years.

I have had the privilege of seeing the learning practices I talk about in this book lived out in the flesh, when I attended training sessions by Robert Fritz, Robert Putnam, and Roger Schwarz. These men truly walk the talk and can manifest that which they are teaching in real time. They gave me the confidence to test out that which I was thinking about to confirm that it actually could work.

John Shibley was the first one to encourage me in this pursuit of thinking and writing. His positive feedback to me when I adapted his Learning Action Matrix diagram helped me recognize that I may have an aptitude for this kind of thinking.

FOR THOSE WHO IMPROVE MY WRITING

I often think in the language of diagrams. Things sometimes just don't make sense until I have created a visual manifestation of them, often in quite a complex manner. Nancy Daugherty, the production manager on this project, has meticulously reproduced my diagrams in a clear and compelling fashion, and for that I am grateful.

I also want to thank Martha Wetherill, who propped the book up a notch with her skillful editing assistance. Her reaction to the content itself gave me some of the first clues that I may be on to something.

My first contact with Janice Molloy, the Content Director at Pegasus Communications, occurred over six years ago, when I submitted a two-page, one-idea article for potential publication in *The Systems Thinker*. Janice impressed me with her editing skill on that humble work, and then with three other articles on which we have subsequently collaborated. She was the one who first suggested that a workbook might be possible. I admire Janice's keen understanding of what I'm trying to articulate, and her ability to organize the text into alternative forms. It has been another great partnership working together on project number five. I truly appreciate her.

FOR THOSE WHOSE COMPANY I KEEP

I want to thank the amazing people at Gerber Memorial Health Services in Fremont, Michigan. This book would not exist if it were not for them. They took a chance by hiring a knower like me and provided a place for nine years of "recovery" work. Because of the freedom and trust given to me by Sue Nieboer, Gary Allore, and Ned Hughes, I was able to practice and play with the ideas contained in this book as part of my organizational development work. I can only hope that the employees of Gerber Memorial have benefited from this work as much as I have.

I also want to thank my fellow GMHS leaders, who submitted to my monthly training sessions, challenged my inconsistencies, and tolerated my weaknesses. Additionally, thanks go out to the members of the various teams I have facilitated, participated in, and learned from: Learning Organization Strategic Team (LOST), Administrative Staff, Strategic Council, Education Council, Culture Crew, Learning...To Lead, Triple-Loop Council, process improvement teams, Suburbans, Conversation Coaches, and many more.

I am especially grateful to my thinking partners Barb Wainright and Jan Stone. From the very early stages of this project, they have given me a forum within which I could test my ideas, and receive support.

I cannot end without acknowledging the contribution my family has given. Being without a father and husband on weekends and evenings is a sacrifice they generously made. My love and thanks go out to Calvin, Brea, Hope, Elise, and Faith.

Introduction

Authors who write books of this genre always presume to have some sort of knowledge they want to impart to their readers. This book is no exception. However, this book, which emphasizes the pitfalls of acting like a knower, presents a special challenge for me. I must somehow share my knowledge without coming across as a knower myself—the very thing that could invalidate what I am trying to relate. Therefore, I begin this book with a confession.

Confession of a Recovering Knower

I am a recovering knower. I am still addicted to knowing but am on the road to a more productive way of being. I started knowing at an early age, and was praised and rewarded for knowing more than my peers. In first grade, my friend Diane and I got attention for being the first ones to get through all the SRA Language Arts modules, one of many early memories that reinforce my fondness for being right and sure. I can still recall how cocky I felt during the Language Arts portion of our days. Gradually, and without knowing it at the time, I began to define myself as a knower.

There were moments when I realized I couldn't maintain my lead ahead of others in my achievement, so I would quit that activity and redefine it as "not important." If I could not be the best at something, I wasn't going to play the game. As a boy with a high level of athletic ability, I would compete every year to earn the Presidential Physical Fitness Award, which I would always attain without too much difficulty. In one event, the 600-yard dash, I had the best time in my class, an honor that I held with quiet pride. One year, I missed school the day we were supposed to complete that event, so, instead of running it with the group, I had to run it alone some days later. I vividly remember having a bit of a panic attack about two-thirds of the way around the course, when I was gripped by the thought that I wasn't running fast enough to get the best time in my class. I was scared that I wouldn't be seen as the fastest 600-yard-dash runner in the sixth grade.

Instead of completing the race as best I could and finding out how fast I had actually run (for I really had no idea), I staged a dramatic "accidental" tripping incident. The loose sand I was running through seemingly shot up and grabbed me by the ankles, making me fall flat on my face and ruining my chance at getting the best time. I straggled over the finish line, feeling sorry for myself and complaining that it's impossible to get a good time running on a course like *that* one. I realize now that I was acting like a knower, big time. I wanted to be perceived as the one who knew how to run the best—anything less was a blow to my self-esteem, something I was not willing to accept.

My knowing in various academic and non-academic settings continued all the way through graduate school and eventually into my first few jobs. Even as it continued to grow, I felt my knowing was under control. I was young and had the stamina to study late into the night and still work the next day—exploits for which I received recognition from my peers. Sometimes, I would secretly go out and study a subject, even in the middle of the work day, just to control a conversation better, appear as if I knew all along, or protect myself from admitting that I really didn't know what to do next.

Being a knower started out as a harmless way to get noticed and applauded, but it continued as a habit that complicated my life. The internal pressure increased to keep providing the right answers. I sometimes took panicked action in an attempt to maintain the appearance of effectiveness. I sensed that something wasn't right, but I never recognized that being a knower was hurting me. And besides, everyone else was doing it, too. To admit that you were wrong or didn't know something, in certain settings, was like sounding a death knell for your career.

Being a knower finally caught up with me, though, when I lost a job in part because I was a knower and not a learner. I was the administrative director of a nonprofit organization, and I supervised a woman who underperformed, played solitaire, and slept on the job. I tried six different methods to improve her performance, all without success. I could not fire her without the consent of the personnel committee and the full board, both of which would not even consider my perspective on this issue, despite multiple attempts. Instead, the board launched a "fact-finding" inquiry, culminating in a final determination meeting. After being shut down in several previous meetings, I was pleased to finally be able to tell my side of the story at that meeting; but when I arrived, I discovered that it had already been adjourned, and three designated board members stayed behind and relieved me of my position on the spot.

I had done everything I could think of to improve my situation—having open and honest conversations, collecting and studying data, experimenting with different tools and techniques, attending workshops, reading books, seeking advice and counsel. But there was one thing I did not try: increasing my willingness to be influenced. I spent a lot of time and effort busily accumulating all this information, really, just so that I might influence others. I attempted to protect myself and focus on my little piece of that world, and didn't reflect on the bigger picture. I tried to shape groups to conform and comply with my notions. In short, I displayed classic knower behaviors.

In my next job, as organizational development facilitator for Gerber Memorial Health Services, one of my responsibilities was to teach leaders the five disciplines of organizational learning from Peter Senge's well-known book, *The Fifth Discipline*. As a good knower, I set out to learn all that I could about the disciplines, determined to grasp just a little more than my students. But a funny thing happened—I actually *learned* this material. And by "learned," I don't mean I merely accumulated more information in my head to use as ammunition at a later time (which is what knowers think of as learning); I mean I increased my ability to produce desired results. I tried out the disciplines, and, to my amazement, they actually made a difference in my life at work and at home.

Through the discipline of personal mastery, I learned how to clarify and pursue the desired results I wanted in my life. Through the discipline of shared vision, I learned to mutually commit to a common aspiration with my coworkers and bring our overall organizational direction into alignment. With systems thinking, I learned to recognize my contribution to the problems I was facing and to see issues from the perspectives of the "whole system" and "underlying structures." The discipline of mental models prepared me to risk having productive conversations with others and to "see" my own thoughts and beliefs. And, finally, by practicing team learning, I was able to subordinate my personal agenda to a larger collective will.

Prior to learning the five disciplines, I would prepare for leading a meeting by studying the subject matter to be discussed, determining for myself the likely outcome, and becoming a superficial "expert" in that subject. Then, when the conversation moved to the place I predicted it would, I hit others hard with my "wisdom." If my prediction for the direction of the conversation was in error, then when the meeting ended, I would get busy researching where the next discussion would likely head and prepare to "impart my wisdom" again. The point here is not that it's bad to prepare for a meeting in this way—for in many instances it actually served the group well. The point is that I did this preparation in a secret way and (partly) for the benefit of looking good. That is what knowers do.

I don't do that anymore. I still research material that may be helpful to a group, but I don't hide the fact that I didn't know it at first, that I put a great deal of effort into acquiring that information, that the depth with which I "know" it is superficial, and that mine may not be the "right" answer, so we should explore the topic further. It may be difficult to see the profoundness of this shift from a single example, but it has freed and empowered me to act more authentic in all that I do. It takes a lot of extra energy to keep all the secrets that a knower has to keep.

In this book, I will describe how to use various learning practices to overcome the "secrets of a knower." This material comes out of my own journey to overcome my addiction to knowing. It is my hope to articulate it in such a way that you will find it helpful on your journey from knower to learner as well.

Learning and a Learning Culture

This book is all about learning and attempting to become more of a learner. It is difficult for you to do so in isolation from other people. You have the best chance of becoming a learner in the context of a "learning culture." A learning culture, as the term is used in this book, includes many of the characteristics of the organizational learning philosophy articulated by Peter Senge in *The Fifth Discipline*. The description of a learning culture that I am fond of is one that has floated around Gerber Memorial for some time; the author is unknown:

> A learning culture is a place where people seek to learn rather than know. They admit that their pictures of the world are incomplete, and therefore they need to learn from each other in order to

> fully understand the whole system. They do this through a process of respectful inquiry into each other's world views. It is a place where people collectively enhance their ability to continually transform themselves and create their desired results.

Organizations or groups with a learning culture have these characteristics in common:

- People have a high-quality experience at work.
- Employees have a deep sense of purpose and alignment.
- There is a strong commitment to telling the truth about current reality.
- There is genuine caring for the organization and for one another.
- People in the organization are growing as persons.
- Employees see how things are connected to one another.

Becoming a learner and developing a learning culture both require transformation and are connected in a symbiotic relationship. As Senge says, "Personal change and organizational change are two sides of the same coin. And the fantasy that we often carry around that somehow my organization will change without me changing is crazy!" (Peter Senge, "Senge on Change and Learning"). The tools, exercises, and ideas presented in this book are designed to destroy the illusion that we can remain the same, as individuals and as organizations, and still produce the results we truly desire.

When I use the word "learning," I have a particular meaning in mind. "Learning has lost its central meaning in contemporary usage," writes Senge. "Learning has become synonymous with 'taking in information.'" However, it would not make sense to say that you have just read several books on horse riding and therefore you've learned how to ride a horse. Senge says that a more accurate understanding of learning would be "to become able to do something we were never able to do"—to achieve what you weren't previously able to achieve. The point of learning is to increase your knowledge, so that you might use it to be more effective in the world.

From this perspective, knowledge is not just the accumulation of information, skills, and experiences, though those are important. Knowledge, as used in this book, is "the ability to produce desired results." Therefore, learning is "increasing one's ability to produce desired results." As Peter Block, best-selling author and consultant, has said, "Learning and performing will become one and the same thing. Everything you say about learning will be about performance. People will get the point that learning is everything" (Peter Block, "The Future of Workplace Learning and Performance").

So, the overall objective of this book is to stimulate you to become a learner, in the full sense of that word. You cannot truly be a learner and remain the same person you were when you started this journey.

This book is designed for front-line practitioners, middle managers, top executives, functional leaders, specialists, consultants—anyone with a vested interest in increasing his or her ability to produced desired results, especially in the context of a learning culture. The practices and frameworks described in this material will serve as an accelerator, or catalyst, for anyone who already possesses the rare combination of burning desire to achieve better results and humble willingness to be influenced. And if you do not yet possess these combined qualities, then you have the right book in your hands too, for developing these qualities is what we will work on together.

Organization of This Book

To help you move from knower to learner, Chapter 1 builds an overall framework to guide you in improving your effectiveness in the world through understanding how learning actually works. Then Chapter 2 explains the concepts of change and learning. In essence, you will be answering the question, "Why should I care about learning, anyway?" The short answer: Your world is changing at an ever-increasing rate, and in order to cope with the challenges and be effective in an environment like this, you will need to learn. Learning is the antidote to unwanted change. Chapter 3 walks you through an explanation of knowers and learners, and how to tell the difference between the two. This may trigger you to wonder if maybe, just maybe, you have some knower inclinations, too. In Chapter 4, you find out by doing five activities that will give you a feel for where your tendencies lie along the knower-learner continuum. Chapter 5 explores "the Learner's Path." Understanding this underlying process of learning is fundamental to discovering what triggers this bias we all have to act like knowers instead of learners. Chapter 6 delves deeper into understanding knower behaviors by exploring a set of thinking habits, called "secrets of a knower." In Chapter 7, you figure out how to overcome these secrets. This discussion will connect you to some of the tools and methods of organizational learning. Then, at the climax of our journey, Chapter 8 pulls it all together by combining structure, behavior, and practical tools to map out the next stage of your knower-to-learner adventure. Finally, Chapter 9 concludes the book by discussing how you can go beyond merely using this material to *become* a learner and start using it *as* a learner.

Connecting with the Author

I welcome your reactions to the material presented in this book. I commit this work to the worldwide community of learners and, in so doing, expect to continue exchanging ideas as our knowledge of learning develops. Let's stay in touch. You can reach me by visiting www.learnerspath.com.

Chapter 1
A New View of Learning

Last week, I had a long conversation with my fifteen-year-old daughter, Elise, about why she had to learn algebra. I had helped her with a complex problem that neither one of us could understand at first. After much consternation, frustration, and finally relief, Elise stumbled upon a related concept that helped her solve the problem at hand. Then she asked, "Do you ever use algebra now that you are an adult?" "No, not the complex type of problems we were just working on," I admitted. "Then why do I have to learn this stuff, if I'll never use it again?" she implored. "It's not useful!"

This exchange brings into sharp contrast the two different definitions of learning that we were operating under. For Elise, learning algebra meant acquiring information in her head about how to manipulate numbers and symbols according to prescribed rules in order to give an answer that would be deemed correct by someone in authority. My definition of learning, in contrast, involved increasing the ability to achieve desired results. Learning *had* to be practically useful—it *had* to lead to outcomes in the real world. To me, what Elise was doing wasn't learning at all: She was simply storing information that she may or may not ever retrieve again (she has no interest in pursuing a career in math or science). So if what she was doing really wasn't learning, why *did* I want her to learn algebra? For a while, I really wasn't quite sure. How was studying algebra going to help Elise achieve her desired results?

In a moment of inspired brilliance (or so *I* thought), I conjured up three reasons why she should learn algebra: (1) It increases brain development by making new neural connections; (2) It helps her acquire intellectual discipline; and (3) It increases her maturity. She was having a hard time relating to these noble, idealized reasons. Then as an afterthought, I added a fourth: It helps her do better on her college entrance exams. Now, I had her attention. She saw a practical use for algebra after all.

As the story above illustrates, we need a more robust perspective of learning than we've had in the past. In this chapter, I am advocating for an integrated framework that describes a new way to understand, utilize, and sustain learning—and, in turn, achieve our desired results.

Human Efficacy

At its most fundamental level, this book shows you how to be more effective. This, in turn, will enable you to achieve small, large, or even your ultimate goals in life. The ultimate aim of humans can be boiled down into three basic categories:

- Seeking fulfillment (pursuing happiness, consciousness, meaning)
- Creating relationships (giving and receiving love, strengthening connection to other people or a higher being)
- Having a purpose (pursuing a dream, fighting for justice, improving the world)

We cannot achieve these aims or our day-to-day goals (e.g., shaving, buying groceries, getting your kids to school on time, serving people in need) without a certain level of human efficacy.

Figure 1-1

Human Efficacy and Ultimate Aims

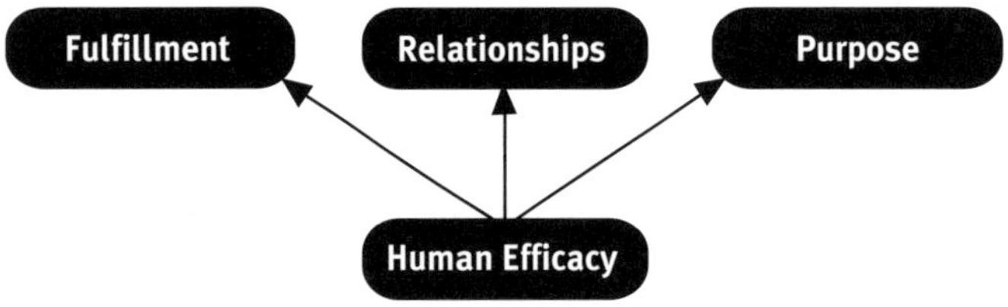

Efficacy is being able to produce a desired effect. Some level of effort must be expended, and therefore some effect produced, to attain our goals as humans. (This is not to say that we can achieve all our aims through individual human effort alone. We must work in cooperation with others and in alignment with our sources of influence, authority, or wisdom. However, we cannot fail to exert an effort and expect we are going to get the outcome we're seeking.)

For example, let's say you want to experience more love in your life. How successful would you be if, in order to accomplish this goal, you sit in a chair and wait for the love to come to you? You don't talk to anyone, you don't look at anyone, you don't think about anyone—in reality, all you really *do* is wait. Not very. You will be unable to produce the desired effect. Another example: Will it be possible for you to be more effective in your job if you don't initiate some sort of movement or influence—even if that movement is simply to begin to notice what others are saying or doing? All desires, lofty or modest, will only be reached through some level of human efficacy.

So then, how do you increase your efficacy? Psychologist Albert Bandura argues that there are several sources for increasing our effectiveness.: "They include [1] mastery experiences, [2] seeing people similar to oneself manage task demands successfully, [3] social persuasion that one has the capabilities to succeed in given activities, and [4] inferences from somatic and emotional states indicative of personal strengths and vulnerabilities." Bandura goes on to say that "the most effective way of creating a strong sense of efficacy is through mastery experiences" (Albert Bandura, "Self-Efficacy," in *Encyclopedia of Human Behavior*). In other words, you build efficacy by repeatedly achieving your desired results.

Figure 1-2

Achieving Results and Human Efficacy

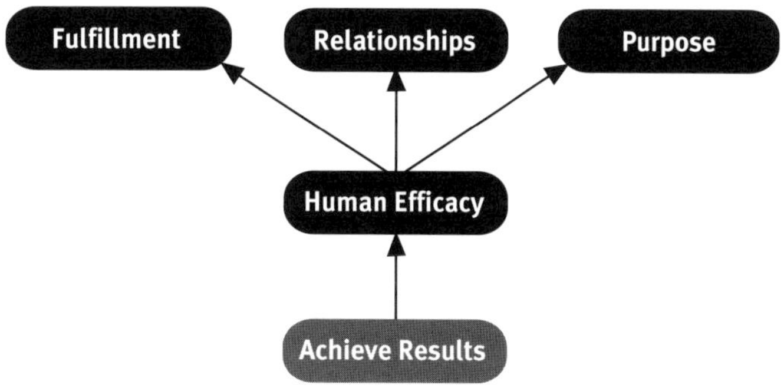

The next question, naturally, is, "How do you get better at 'repeatedly achieving your desired results'?" The answer is *learning*. Unfortunately, without understanding how learning actually works, most of us are less than intentional about how we learn. And, consequently, we take actions that are unconscious, random, or undirected, at worst, or ineffective, at best. Therefore, the next section will attempt to provide that important understanding.

How Learning Works

In the most concise, generic form I can express, learning works like this:

First, you become aware of a discrepancy between "the way things are" and "the way things ought to be"—you realize that you are not achieving desired results.

Second, you make a choice to address the discrepancy and decide that something has to change. Your response emerges either out of a *knower* stance, which says someone or something else will have to change (a focus on the *circumstances*) or a *learner* stance, which says *you* will have to change (a focus on your *ability to respond* to the circumstances).

If you decide to respond out of a knower stance, you will (eventually) become ineffective. New and different challenges and circumstances confront you daily. Responding to tomorrow's dynamic challenges with your current, static abilities will, over time, lose its effectiveness.

Third, you choose to respond out of the learner stance and decide that *you* will have to change. So, you will take actions to increase your ability to respond to the circumstances you are facing. If your ability to respond becomes greater than the circumstances, you will achieve positive results, but if the circumstances remain greater than your ability to respond, then you will get negative results.

Because learning can be difficult, we all, unfortunately, have a tendency to respond from the knower stance. Making a change requires a direct confrontation with the status quo. And in confronting the status quo, you will eventually discover that your ability to respond is less than you'd like it to be, and this discovery, in turn, may generate feelings of threat or embarrassment. So, in order to protect yourself, you take the stance that someone or something else (i.e., the

Figure 1-3

A New View of Learning

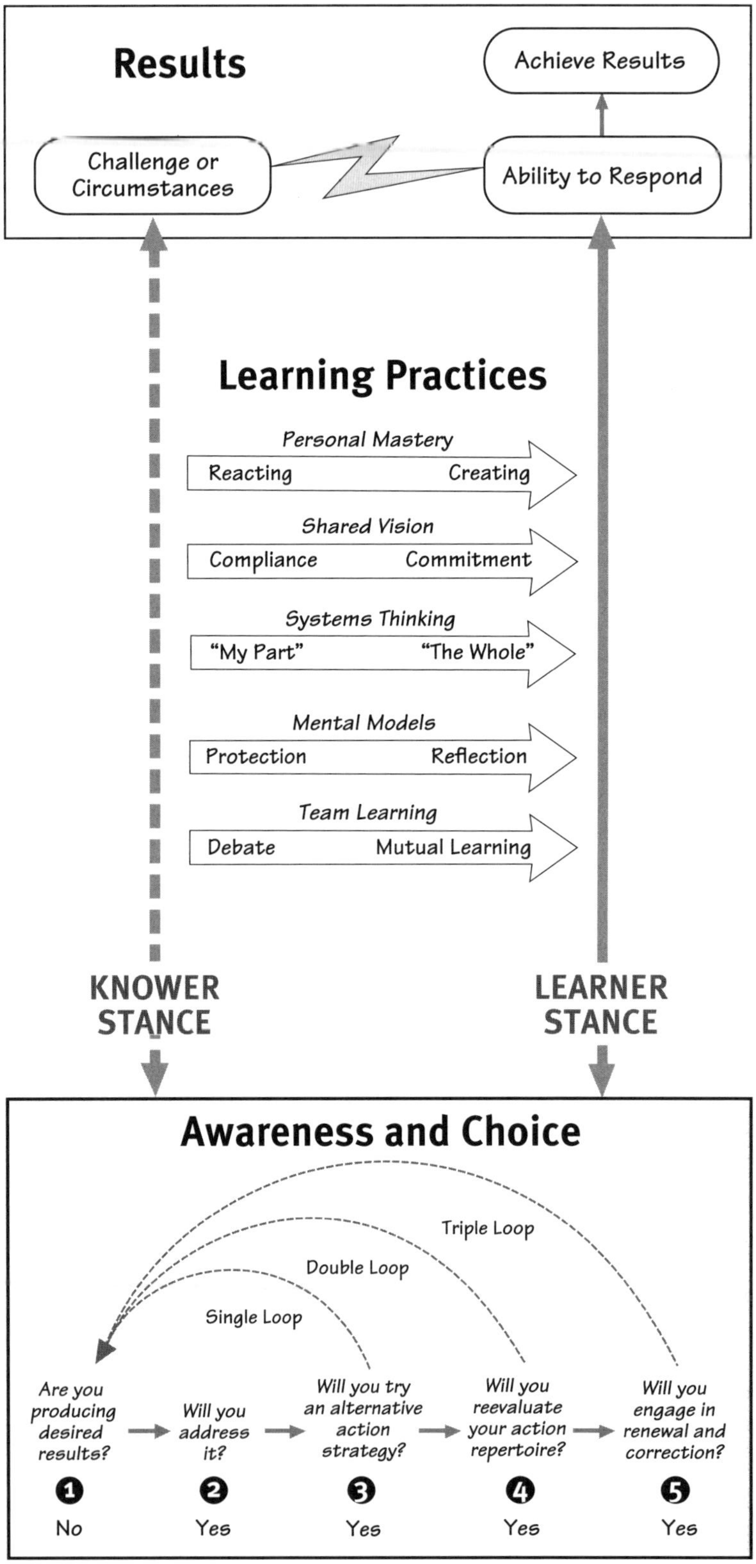
Results
Achieve Results
Challenge or Circumstances
Ability to Respond
Learning Practices
Personal Mastery
Reacting
Creating
Shared Vision
Compliance
Commitment
Systems Thinking
"My Part"
"The Whole"
Mental Models
Protection
Reflection
Team Learning
Debate
Mutual Learning
KNOWER STANCE
LEARNER STANCE
Awareness and Choice
Triple Loop
Double Loop
Single Loop
Are you producing desired results?
Will you address it?
Will you try an alternative action strategy?
Will you reevaluate your action repertoire?
Will you engage in renewal and correction?
1
No
2
Yes
3
Yes
4
Yes
5
Yes

circumstances) must change. Over time, you become so skilled at this way of reacting that you assimilate these thinking habits into your everyday practice, and they become your knower stance.

Fourth, you will vigilantly notice whenever you are responding out of a knower stance and choose to shift back into the learner stance. You will make this shift easier by diligently employing five learning practices: personal mastery, shared vision, mental models, systems thinking, and team learning. A disciplined application of these five learning practices will help you continually look at yourself as the necessary focus of change and increase your ability to respond appropriately and achieve your desired results.

AWARENESS AND CHOICE

Many times, the choices we make are hidden from our conscious awareness. For example, when I first got married, I was in the habit of pointing out the flaws in my wife's suggestions when she proposed an idea with which I disagreed. I figured I was just helping her to "think things through a little more clearly," when in reality all I was doing was frustrating her to no end. It wasn't until she pointed out that all I ever did was poke holes in her ideas, without making an alternative suggestion of my own, that I became aware of how my behavior was unfair to her. When I became consciously aware of how I was acting, I could choose to continue with it (perhaps more skillfully, so as not to get caught quite so often), or I could choose to change my behavior, so that it was more productive and caring.

We go through life, to a great extent, unaware of the choices we are making. To be more effective in the world, it is important to consciously operate from a learner stance. So we need a way to wake up our awareness about which stance we are living out of, so we can then make choices—behave in ways—that are in alignment with the learner stance rather than the knower stance. Learning cannot begin without awareness and cannot continue without the making of fundamental choices. Both of these elements are facilitated through the use of the questions contained in the Learner's Path (see Chapter 5).

KNOWER STANCE VERSUS LEARNER STANCE

The terms "knower" and "learner" will be used throughout this book and discussed in some depth in Chapter 3. For now, though, let's define a knower as someone who can't admit that they don't know something, for fear that doing so will make them look bad. They often pretend that they know things even when they don't, and they are not willing to be influenced. They are like those know-it-all kids we knew in grade school, except that, as adults, they are much better at hiding it when they don't know something. Alternatively, let's define a learner as someone who admits they could be wrong, or that they are uncertain, or that they probably have to change their usual actions in order to achieve their desired results. Learners are willing to be influenced.

Whether you adopt the knower stance or the learner stance depends on how you answer the three questions depicted in the Stance Decision Tree (Figure 1-4). If you believe you are actually "getting what you want," you will take on a non-learner stance—there is no need for learning, things are fine, nothing needs to

Figure 1-4

Stance Decision Tree

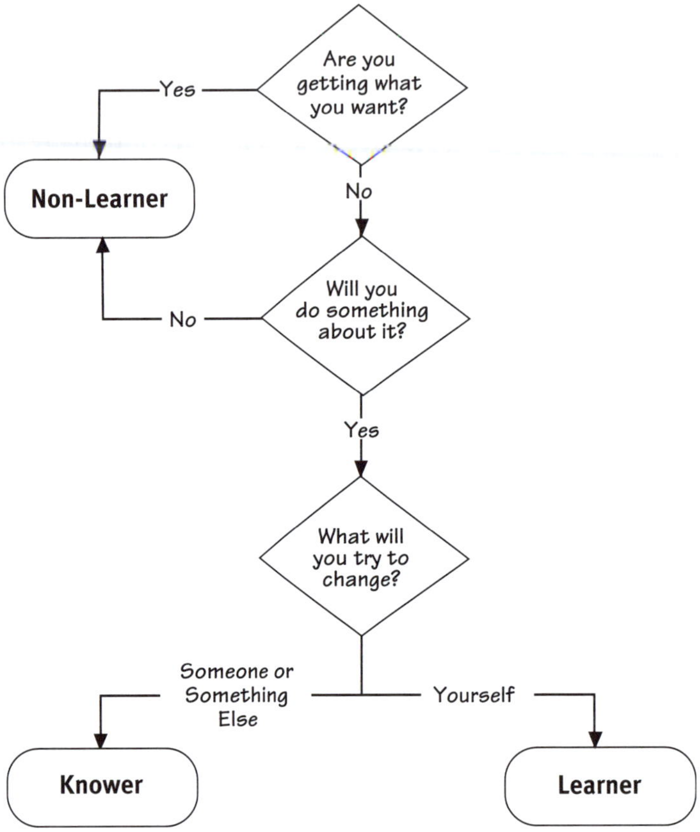

change. If, however, you believe you are *not* getting what you want, but you don't want to do something about that discrepancy, then you will, likewise, take on the non-learner stance.

If you believe that you are not getting what you want *and* you decide that you will do something about it, your next choice is "What will you try to change?" If you attempt to change someone or something else (focus on the circumstances), you are living out of the knower stance, and if you attempt to change yourself (focus on improving your ability to respond), you are living out of the learner stance.

For example, let's say you become aware that your accounting practices are peppered with errors rather than being the pristine example of proper accounting you thought they were. You are now faced with a choice. How will you address what is happening? If you focus attention on someone or something else, such as why no one ever told you this before, or how you had received poor training in accounting, or how this was fine at the place you used to work, then you are taking a knower stance. On the other hand, if you focus attention on yourself, such as feeling stuck in a rut, or not staying up-to-date on the latest techniques, or lacking passion for doing accounting in the first place, then you are choosing a learner stance. You can tell whether people have taken a learner stance or a knower stance based on where they primarily focus their attention (this is illustrated by the two vertical lines in Figure 1-3). If they persistently focus their attention on changing someone or something else, they are living from the knower stance; if they persistently focus on changing themselves, then they have taken a learner stance.

RESULTS

In baseball, home plate is the most important place on the diamond. A run is scored when a player rounds the bases and touches home plate, and not before. It is the central focus of the action—the ball must always be thrown to it or hit from it.

Likewise, achievement of results is the home plate of learning. All learning must be directed to achievement of results or emerge from it. There is no learning without achieving desired results. As explained in greater detail in Chapter 3, and illustrated at the top of Figure 1-3, results occur through the interaction of (1) the challenge or circumstances we face and (2) our ability to successfully respond to the challenge. When our ability to respond is greater than the challenge itself, then results will be positive; and when the challenge is greater than our ability to respond, we will get negative results.

Let's bring the baseball analogy a little further. Think of the pitcher as the circumstances or challenges you must face, and think of yourself, and your ability to respond, as the batter. The pitcher hurls challenge after challenge at you. If your ability to respond is greater than the circumstances, you will hit the ball, but if the circumstances are greater than your ability to respond, you will miss the ball or watch it fly past.

The most effective people are always increasing their ability to respond to the changes and challenges they face, and thereby keeping the ratio of "challenge" to "ability to respond" tilted in their favor. On the other hand, when faced with challenging circumstances, less effective people focus their attention on the circumstances rather than increasing their ability to respond. So they blame the circumstances, avoid the circumstances, cover up the circumstances, deny that the circumstances are as bad as they seem, or blame someone or something else *for* the circumstances.

As an *effective* baseball player, you would continually seek to increase your ability to hit the ball, no matter who the pitcher is or what type of pitch he is throwing. If you began to frequently strike out, you would focus on your inability to respond and ask, "What part of my hitting needs to improve in order to hit what is being pitched to me?" As an *ineffective* player, frequently striking out, you would start to question the circumstances (e.g., the umpire isn't fair; the sun is in my eyes; at least I haven't struck out as many times as Carlos; I've got the wrong bat; etc.) rather than your ability to respond (hitting ability).

You cannot achieve your desired results by focusing attention exclusively on the circumstances rather than on your ability to respond to those circumstances. It doesn't make sense to ignore the circumstances, however, for they are part of the equation of effectiveness. In fact, you must explore and interact with them. But then you must redirect your energy toward developing the ability to respond successfully *to* those circumstances.

Learning begins and ends with achievement of desired results. You cannot know whether you have actually learned anything unless and until you compare the results you are getting with those that you desire to achieve.

FIVE CORE LEARNING PRACTICES

As you become more skillful at catching yourself reacting from the knower stance and, simultaneously, desiring to live more out of the learner stance, you will recognize a need to develop your learning muscles, or your capacity for learning. In order to do so, you will need to practice five fundamental learning disciplines (as Peter Senge described in *The Fifth Discipline*)—personal mastery, shared vision, mental models, systems thinking, and team learning. (See Chapter 7, where these are explained in detail.) As you develop your learning muscles in each of the five disciplines, you will progress along five continuums from a "knower" to a "learner" (illustrated by horizontal arrows in Figure 1-3).

As you practice the disciplines, there is a developmental process—a progression away from knower behaviors toward learner behaviors. While there is some risk of labeling people by using such words as "knower" and "learner," these terms are used in this context as convenient handles to suggest a contrast between "where we are" in our learning journey and "where we want to end up." You might think of them like those "before" and "after" photographs often used in weight-loss advertisements. You don't have much of an appreciation for the "after" picture unless it's contrasted with the "before" picture. Likewise, you don't much appreciate what it takes to become a learner unless it's contrasted with living like a knower. This framework is meant to imply that you cannot stay the same and remain effective in you life.

There are many, many learning practices that you can use, including meditation, reading, intuition, reflection, suspending assumptions, dialogue, intention, team-building, productive conversations, and so on. The five learning disciplines that are explored here are not the exclusive practices that you need to master to get to learning "heaven." Instead, consider them the core disciplines (along with any associated tools, techniques, or practices) that will help you develop your capacity for deeper and richer learning. Many of the learning practices would serve to enhance and build capacity for progressing along one or more of the learning discipline continuums.

Personal Mastery

If you have transitioned from knower to learner along the personal mastery continuum, you will have felt an internal shift from external pressure to internal desire. Formerly, you reacted to external pressures and expectations defined for you by someone or something else, but now you experience an intense internal desire to create the results you truly want in your life. You have developed the ability to *bring something new into existence.*

Shared Vision

As an advanced practitioner of shared vision, you have shifted from controlling group interactions with a goal of getting compliance from the members to facilitating mutual commitment. You have developed the ability to *co-create collective aspiration.*

Mental Models

As someone operating from the learner end of the mental models continuum, you have given up defending yourself during conversations using "protection mode" and now embrace self-exploration using "reflection mode." You have a well-developed ability to *distinguish between "myself" and "my view."*

Systems Thinking

An experienced practitioner of systems thinking, you have shifted your perspective from focusing exclusively on "my part" to focusing on "the whole." You have a well-developed ability to *see your role in the whole.*

Team Learning

As you have moved from knower to learner along the team learning continuum, you have shifted from directing and debating during group conversations to having group conversations focused on mutual learning. You have a well-developed ability to *generate collective insight.*

Living As a Learner

The ultimate aim of this book is to help you live your life as a learner, both individually and collectively. Living an effective life—whether it is achieving your ultimate aim or swatting at little problems that annoy you—begins and ends with understanding how learning works. With this understanding, you are in a position to make critical choices. Do you want to take actions based on a knower stance or based on a learner stance? If you see yourself avoiding, covering up, or denying the circumstances or blaming someone or something else *for* the circumstances, you know you are living from the knower stance. If you see yourself taking actions designed to change someone or something else, without first focusing on changing yourself, you will, again, recognize that you are mired in the knower stance. If you see yourself creating, reflecting, building commitment, seeing your role in the whole, and engaging in mutual learning, you will be aware that you are living from the learner stance.

Becoming aware, making choices, focusing on your ability to respond, and achieving your desired results—*this* is living your life as a learner.

Rapid Recap

- Efficacy is fundamental to achieving our ultimate aims as humans. You build efficacy by repeatedly achieving your desired results. You get better at "repeatedly achieving your desired results" by learning.
- A new view of learning includes four integrated elements: awareness and choice, knower/learner stance, results, and learning practices.

■ The evidence that you are on the right path is that you are developing the ability to:

- bring new things into existence.
- distinguish between "myself" and "my view."
- see your role in the whole.
- co-create collective aspiration.
- generate collective insight.

Reflective Response

■ When you recognize that you are not achieving desired results, your natural inclination is to:

1. Explain the circumstances/challenge, or focus on changing someone or something else.
2. Examine your own inability to respond, or focus on changing yourself.

- Why do you think this is?

■ To what extent do you practice these core learning capacities?

Bring New Things into Existence	Say What?	Never Tried	Can't Do It	Sometimes Successful	Do It More and More	Do It Regularly and Effortlessly
See Your Role in the Whole	Say What?	Never Tried	Can't Do It	Sometimes Successful	Do It More and More	Do It Regularly and Effortlessly
Distinguish Between "Myself" and "My View"	Say What?	Never Tried	Can't Do It	Sometimes Successful	Do It More and More	Do It Regularly and Effortlessly
Co-create Collective Aspiration	Say What?	Never Tried	Can't Do It	Sometimes Successful	Do It More and More	Do It Regularly and Effortlessly
Generate Collective Insight	Say What?	Never Tried	Can't Do It	Sometimes Successful	Do It More and More	Do It Regularly and Effortlessly

Chapter 2

Learning to Change and Changing to Learn

Most of us experience change as an unwelcome and upsetting guest in our lives. You get miffed when your key no longer opens the door to your usual meeting room, because your boss forgot to mention changing the locks. Or it takes you two or three frustrating days to reprogram the TV after the cable company alters the channel line-up *again*. You feel unsettled and neglected when the library changes its staff schedule and replaces your favorite librarian with a stranger who doesn't know your name. You feel defeated and behind the times when you discover that your competitor down the street now provides themed, customized *experiences* for their customers, while your company has just rolled out new standards and training for consistent customer *service*. And on it goes.

You likely see these challenges as "not the way things are supposed to be," and you may even judge them as "bad." No matter how you see your changing circumstances now, by the end of this book, I hope you see them as "normal" or "usual"—change just *is*. You will learn that you don't resist change; you navigate it. And you can learn to navigate it successfully and gracefully, with an integrated view of change and learning.

It is undeniable that the increasing pace and persistence of change is one of the primary challenges of our everyday existence. Many books about change in society—and about change itself—are published every year. (On the day these words were written, Amazon.com listed 21,323 books under the subject heading of "change"; of those, 2,588 were considered business management and leadership books.)

The rate and frequency of change is captured nicely in the expression "permanent white water," Peter Vaill's phrase from his book, *Learning As a Way of Being*. In it, he describes permanent white water as "the complex, turbulent, changing environment in which we are all trying to operate." He goes on to connect this type of change to the need for learning in order to cope with the challenges before us: "Since turbulent conditions appear everywhere and pervade our lives in both time and space, learning in permanent white water conditions is and will continue to be a constant way of life for all of us."

Peter Drucker magnifies this sentiment in his article, "How Schools Must Change," when he says, "We now accept the fact that learning is a lifelong process of keeping abreast of change. And the most pressing task is to teach people how to learn." There are many others, including politicians, philosophers, spiritual leaders, celebrities, and poets, who have connected change and learning. Learning is the antidote to unwanted change and the prescription for the change you desire.

The Growth Curve

The human response to change has been studied across many academic disciplines. David Elrod and Donald Tippett, in their comparison of various research studies titled "The 'Death Valley' of Change," discovered a similar pattern among people who pursue growth and learning as a way to deal with change. Figure 2-1 shows that when we attempt to make an improvement in our lives, our performance actually degrades for a time and then subsequently improves to an even higher level than when we started. This pattern, called a "growth curve," is a significant part of any learning process.

Figure 2-1

The Death Valley of Change

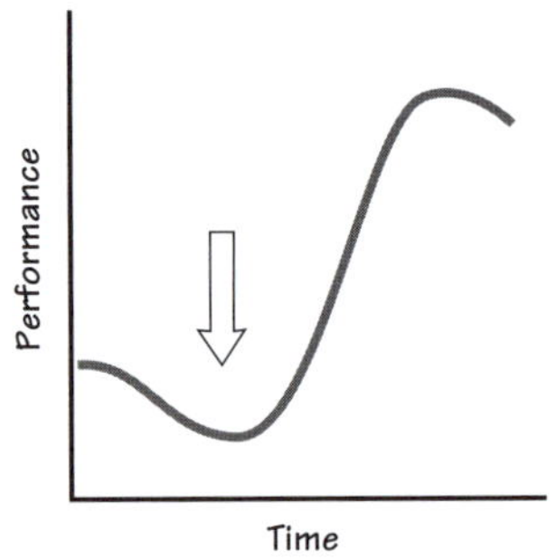

In his book, *Navigating Through Change*, Harry Woodward takes this growth curve to another level of usefulness. Building on the foundational work of George Land and Beth Jarman's *Breakpoint and Beyond*, Woodward outlines three stages of growth and change (see Figure 2-2).

- ***Stage 1: Forming.*** This is the start-up period, when you have decided there is something you want to become, create, or improve. Excitement, energy, and hope prevail in this stage, as well as some frustration and a sense of "three steps forward and two steps back." Being inventive, decisive, committed, and flexible will serve you well in this stage. Behind the experimentation and trial and error exploration lies the basic drive to find a repeatable pattern of success. Consequently, as you are "trying on" different behaviors, performance gets worse before it gets better.

Figure 2-2

Three Stages of Growth

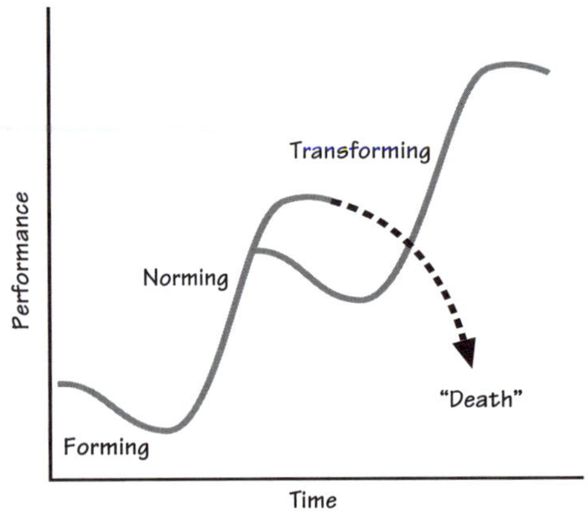

- ***Stage 2: Norming.*** At this point, you or your organization have discovered a repeatable pattern of success. Anything that does not serve to support, extend, or improve the basic pattern is discarded. Instead of opening up to many possibilities, as in Stage 1, here you focus attention on ideas that make this pattern of success more efficient and effective. Incremental improvements are the norm. This is the period when performance picks up and stabilizes, when you feel pride for accomplishments, but may also feel bored or complacent.
- ***Stage 3: Transforming.*** This stage begins when you notice that your performance isn't what it used to be or that it takes more effort to get your usual results. Your first response is to try to extend the second (norming) stage through continued efforts at making incremental changes. Then, over time, you realize that this kind of effort isn't helping you cope with change and that "death," or complete failure, is possible. It is at this point that you switch from a reactive orientation to a creative orientation. You have to create a new system and transform your action strategies. And when you do, you are effectively back at the first stage, forming, again—but this time using new systems, habits, or processes. Here you reconsider ideas that were originally rejected during the second phase. You will again be seeking to discover a new repeatable pattern of success. Meanwhile, the old pattern of success simultaneously flattens out and begins its downward trend toward obsolescence.

Entering the transforming stage is like starting another forming stage, but without the simplicity. This time, you will have to share the environment with the existing, although dying, normative system. You are in the process of replacing the old system with the new system. Consequently, according to Woodward, you can find yourself at any one of six different positions throughout the transforming stage, as illustrated in Figure 2-3.

1. Knocking on the door—just entering the third stage
2. Hanging on—trying to preserve the old order
3. Branching off—attempting new ideas and procedures
4. Reaching the crossroads—reaching the make-or-break point for new ideas
5. Consolidating—normalizing/assimilating the changes
6. Dying on the vine—being unable to transition

Figure 2-3

Positions in the Transforming Stage

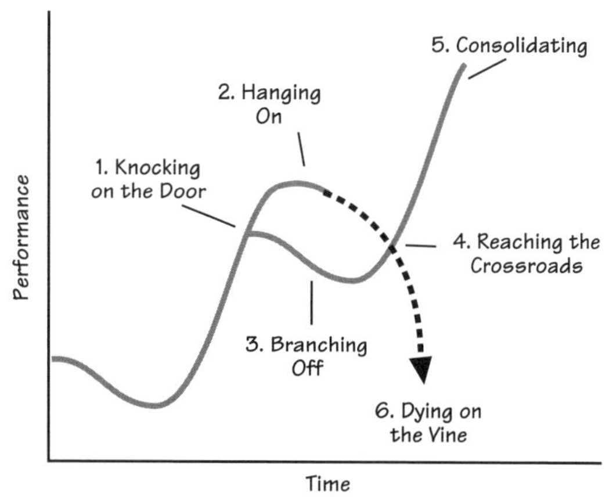

Figure 2-4

The Repeating Pattern of Change

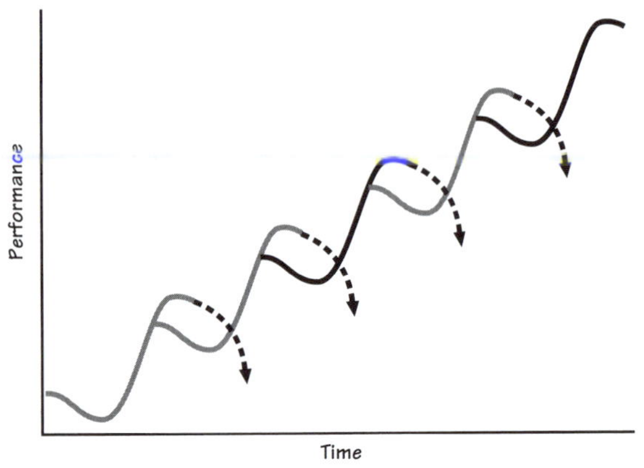

Figure 2-5

Permanent White Water

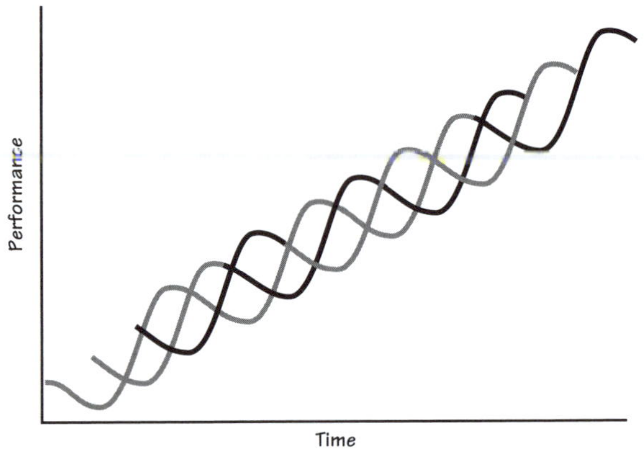

Another adaptation Woodward adds to this model is the pace of change. We have seen how, in the transforming stage, the old process dies out simultaneously as the new process is born. This is not a one-time event; this pattern repeats itself over and over, as shown in Figure 2-4.

Then, as the pace of change quickens even further, the norming stage disappears altogether, as shown in Figure 2-5. This is what permanent white water looks like.

The Three Types of Learning

Living and succeeding in a world of permanent white water requires learning—but not just any kind of learning. There are different types of learning—single-, double-, and triple-loop—and each one can be particularly helpful at certain stages of the growth curve (the terms single- and double-loop learning were coined by Chris Argyris and described in *Overcoming Organizational Defenses*; the pairing of single-, double-, and triple-loop learning with changing your doing, thinking, and being is adapted from Robert Hargrove in *Masterful Coaching*).

All three kinds of learning are understood in terms of cycles, or repeating processes. These three learning cycles link tightly together to complement and build on one another. The core learning cycle contains four basic steps (plus a one-time start-up step). There are many other learning cycle models that you could use, containing greater or fewer steps, and it doesn't really matter which one you choose, as long as it contains both action and reflection steps.

SINGLE-LOOP LEARNING: CHANGING OUR DOING

This learning model (shown in Figure 2-6) starts by defining your desired results in the center of the loop—what is it that you want to increase or improve, and to what extent? After this initial step, which gets the learning cycle going, you can go to any other step and progress in a clockwise direction. For example, start

Figure 2-6

Single-Loop Learning

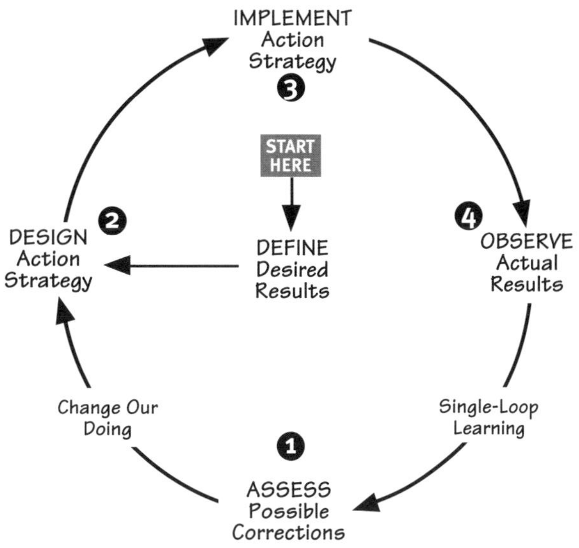

with Step 2, where you would design an action strategy that you believe will get the results that you desire. Then, moving clockwise to Step 3, you implement your action strategy and, at Step 4, observe whether your actions actually got you the results you desired. If they did, great—you've achieved the outcomes you wanted, so no more learning is needed around this issue. If your actions did not achieve your desired results, then you return to Step 1 to assess possible corrections. Here, you'll go back to the drawing board, so to speak, and think about what to do differently next time. After selecting a possible correction, you design another, different action strategy (Step 2), implement it (Step 3), and then observe the results (Step 4) once again. This cycle can continue until you achieve your desired results or have run out of new action strategies to implement.

When I was younger, my favorite sport was waterskiing. I spent a lot of time with my friends experimenting, practicing, and mastering its various forms. Eventually, I became a fairly good barefoot waterskier. One of the tricks my friends and I were trying to master was the tumbleturn, which is executed by skiing along barefoot at 35 to 40 miles per hour, sitting down, and flipping onto your back, spinning around 360 degrees, placing your feet back into position on the water, and standing up to glide along on your feet again. When done by the best skiers, this trick takes a few seconds—feet, back, feet, done.

Reprinted with permission from Jason Tithof.

I spent a whole summer trying to *learn* this trick (remember, "learning" means increasing your ability to produce desired results). My desired result was clear: complete one tumbleturn successfully. I kept that single-loop learning cycle spinning at top speed: I read magazines and books; I studied pictures and illustrations; I discussed every element with my friends; I practiced on land; I attempted the trick to the left, to the right, around a corner, on a straightaway, faster, slower. You name it—I tried it. The end of the story, to my great disapointment, is that I never, ever completed a successful tumbleturn. I made progress but reached the end of my action repertoire. I used "what I knew" to achieve "what I could."

Single-loop learning is an important and necessary type of learning, and we frequently return to it to achieve our desired results. Many times, it is just what we need, and no more. But sometimes, especially after rotating around the single-loop learning cycle a few times, we realize that if we really want to achieve our desired results, we can't just rely on making incremental changes.

DOUBLE-LOOP LEARNING: CHANGING OUR THINKING

While single-loop learning leads you to think about what new actions you might try out next time, it does not ask you to examine or change the overall set of assumptions you were operating under while doing your previous "learning." When single-loop solutions have lost their effectiveness, it is time to learn about your learning. *Double-loop learning* will help you learn about the mental framework you were operating under while doing your single-loop learning. In other words, we can think of single-loop learning as change *within* a particular mental framework and double-loop learning as change *of* that framework.

Figure 2-7

Double-Loop Learning

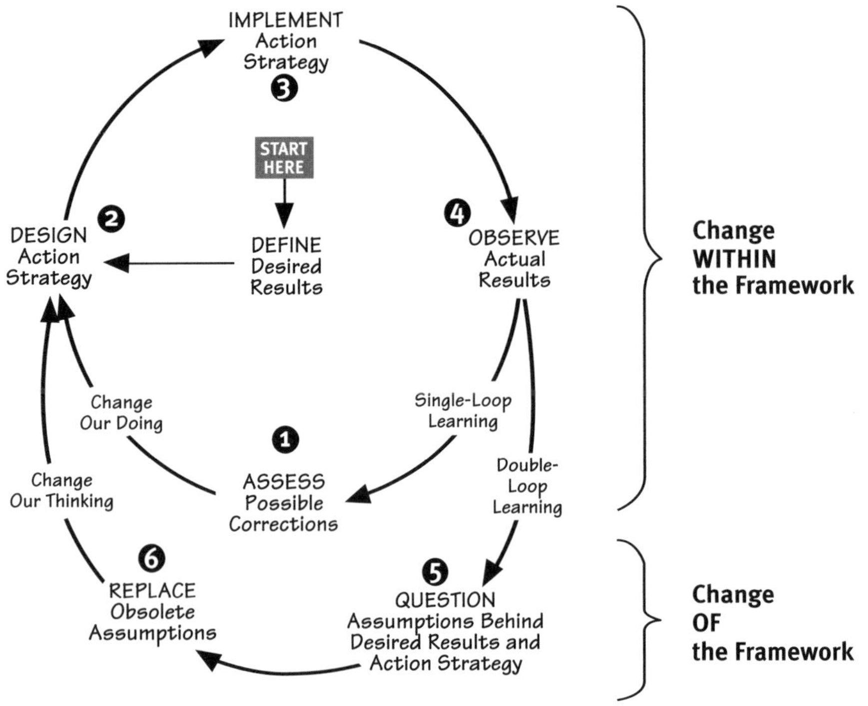

Returning to my tumbleturn example, I realize now (20 years later) that I had exhausted my whole action repertoire as it relates to tumbleturns. It was time for a new, deeper type of learning. In order to expand my action repertoire, I needed to examine and challenge the mental framework under which I was doing my previous "learning" (Step 5 in Figure 2-7). There are two important questions to ask when uncovering your mental framework: (1) Why do you *really* want this desired result? and (2) What made you think that your previous action strategy would work, anyway?

Asking the Double-Loop Questions

In answer to the first question, I wanted the result of being able to do a tumbleturn because it fit in with the image I had of myself—unique, athletic, and adventurous. I also wanted it because my friends could do the trick, and I couldn't, so there was a competitive element to it, too. In answer to the second question, the reason I thought the previous action strategies would work was because I had used this same approach (study, observe, practice constantly) to become proficient at other sports before. I believed I had the physical prowess that I needed.

Replacing Obsolete Assumptions

Once you examine the mental framework around your action repertoire, the next step in double-loop learning is to replace the obsolete assumptions with ones that are more in line with reality (Step 6). I began to see that, in answering the first question, my primary desired result wasn't "nailing a tumbleturn" (and experiencing the joy of bringing my skill to the next level); my true desired result was to "compete with and surpass my friends." Honestly, what hurt most was being the only one who couldn't do the trick. In answering the second question, I began to see that my assumption (that the physical requirements to do a tumbleturn are the same as those required to play soccer or basketball) was inaccurate. I began to understand that I just did not have the upper-body strength needed to do a successful tumbleturn.

Based on the insights of answering these double-loop questions, the next step in double-loop learning is to return to Step 2 to design a new action strategy. So, I figured a reasonable action strategy to pursue at this point would be either of these options:

- Shore up my weakness (literally) by hitting the weights and building my upper-body strength, and then continue to compete with my friends to do tumbleturns, and/or
- Start pursuing a different activity with which to compete with my friends—after all, the point is to beat my friends, not necessarily to enjoy a tumbleturn.

I chose the later of the two options and moved on to compete in other activities. Maybe tumbleturns weren't my thing—maybe there were other waterskiing tricks I could pursue.

TRIPLE-LOOP LEARNING: CHANGING OUR BEING

Sometimes, even after diligent use of both single- and double-loop learning, we are *still* unable to achieve our desired results. It may be time to pursue *triple-loop learning*, which involves deep introspection. The first step of triple-loop learning

Figure 2-8

Triple-Loop Learning

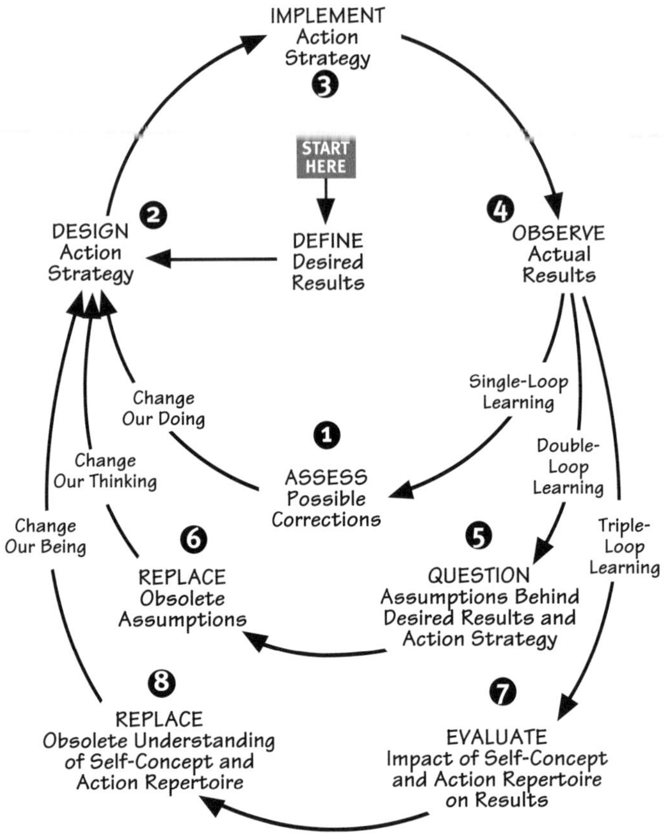

is assessing how your self-concept and your action repertoire either help or hinder you from achieving your desired results (Step 7 in Figure 2-8). As you recall, my new, clarified goal was to compete with and surpass my friends. So if I couldn't achieve that with tumbleturns, maybe there were other activities. After tumbleturns, my friends moved on to barefooting backward. It was beginning to dawn on me that competing in barefoot tricks was not an area in which I could surpass my friends. Did I really want to put myself through the torture of taking on this challenge when I would likely have nothing much to show for it except a head full of water and a battered body? So now I would need to ask myself a couple of triple-loop questions: (1) What impact is my self-concept having on my ability to achieve my desired results? and (2) How is my action repertoire affecting my ability to achieve my desired results?

Asking the Triple-Loop Questions

As I said earlier, the self-concept I was trying to maintain while waterskiing was as a "unique, athletic, and adventurous" person who can surpass his friends. Unique, athletic, and adventurous persons would never back down, would always compete with their friends, and would always beat their bodies to a pulp, because that's what unique, athletic, adventurous people do. So I recognized that the need to maintain my self-concept would cause me to pursue things I didn't enjoy and wasn't that good at.

The other triple-loop issue I faced was that my action repertoire was tempting me to pursue backward barefooting with my friends. My approach consisted of studying, observing, and then practicing like crazy, relying on my natural athletic ability to pull me through. You've probably heard the saying, "When all you have is a hammer, everything looks like a nail." Backward barefooting looked like just another nail that I could pound on with this same physical action repertoire.

Replacing Obsolete Understandings

The next step of triple-loop learning is to replace your obsolete understandings of your self-concept and your action repertoire (Step 8). Again, making these kinds of changes is deep and personal work that usually takes a long time to implement—anywhere from several months to a lifetime. In my case, I eventually replaced my old self-concept of "a competitive physical adventurer" with one of "a non-competitive mental adventurer."

I expanded my action repertoire beyond the physical realm to the mental realm over the years. Through a series of setbacks and surprises, I discovered a few areas of mental prowess I never knew I had until I went through the often unpleasant process of triple-loop learning. My desired results have changed along the way—from the need to complete physical tricks to a desire to pursue learning adventures with others.

Navigating Change with the Three Types of Learning

Now that you are familiar with both the three stages of the growth curve and the three types of learning, let's take a look at how to interweave them to help you learn and, consequently, navigate change successfully.

STAGE 1: FORMING

If we think of single-loop learning as *changing our doing*, then it is the most beneficial type of learning in the first stage of the growth curve. In the forming stage,

Figure 2-9

Three Types of Learning on a Growth Curve

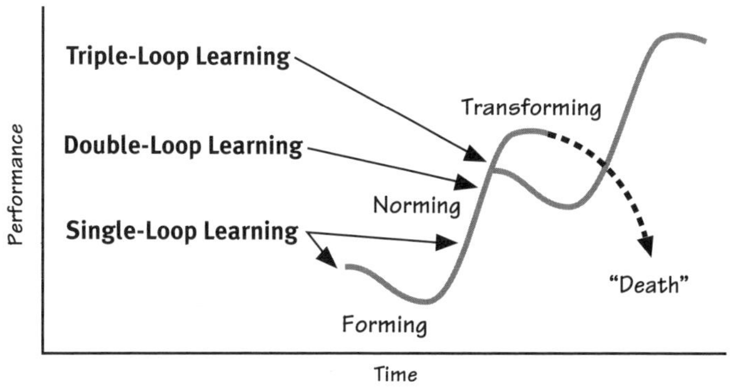

we are trying this, trying that, and trying that other thing. We are looking for a repeatable pattern of success. It does not yet exist, so applying double- or triple-loop learning is premature.

STAGE 2: NORMING

In this stage, you no longer look for new patterns of success but optimize the patterns already discovered. In other words, you exploit what works and make it work even better. Single- and double-loop learning fit nicely here, because we want to constantly improve and extend the longevity of the norming stage. Single-loop learning is especially relevant early on, when we just need to tweak things to maintain momentum, and double-loop learning is especially valuable in the later part of this stage, when we haven't lost confidence in the success pattern, but we need to revamp it to make it fit the shifting context.

STAGE 3: TRANSFORMING

In order to enter this stage, you must have a double- or triple-loop learning insight. By definition, the transforming stage is a break from the past success pattern (which isn't looking very promising anymore), and that break is *initiated by* reflecting on your thinking (double-loop) or reflecting on your being (triple-loop).

This chapter opens with the position that learning is the antidote to unwanted change. Many people do not respond to such challenges, but instead hide from or try to ignore them. Eventually, this practice will present a problem for them. As you will see in the next chapter, when we awaken to the fact that we are no longer achieving our desired results, we must make a choice between a learner stance and a knower stance.

Rapid Recap

- The increasing pace and persistence of change is one of the primary challenges of our everyday existence.
- Learning is the antidote to unwanted change and the prescription for desired change.
- There are three stages of successful change/growth: forming, norming, and transforming.
- We can broadly describe single-loop learning as "changing your doing," double-loop learning as "changing your thinking," and triple-loop learning as "changing your being."
- Single-loop learning is particularly relevant for the forming and norming stages of the change/growth curve, while double- and triple-loop learning are necessary for the transforming stage.

Reflective Response

- Can you identify various areas in your life where you are experiencing each of the three different stages of change/growth?
    - ***Forming:*** In what area(s) of your life are you trying out multiple action strategies but haven't yet discovered that "repeatable pattern of success"?
    - ***Norming:*** In what area(s) of your life have you found that repeatable pattern of success and are rejecting alternative action strategies?
    - ***Transforming:*** In what area(s) are desired results harder to come by than they used to be, and the usual methods seem to have lost some of their power?
- Can you recall examples of single-, double-, and triple-loop learning from various points in your life?
    - I described my triple-loop insight of replacing my old self-concept of a "competitive physical adventurer" with a new one of a "non-competitive mental adventurer." Can you think of a time when you had a triple-loop insight related to your self-concept?

Chapter 3

Knowers and Learners

In the TV show, *The Office*, the character of Michael Scott, regional manager of Dunder Mifflin Paper Supply Company, is the personification of a "knower." His self-concept is so tied to knowing the right answers and looking like a leader ought to look that, when he calls a staff meeting to address rumors about downsizing, he acts and speaks with bravado, when inwardly he feels panicked and desperate.

Michael: Now, I know there's some rumors out there, and I just kinda want to set the record straight. Corporate has deemed it appropriate to enforce an ultimatum upon me. And Jan [Corporate V.P.] is thinking about downsizing either the Stanford branch or this branch. And let me assure you that it isn't going to be this branch.

Oscar: Yeah, but Michael, what if they downsize here.

Michael: Not gonna happen.

Stanley: It could be out of your hands, Michael.

Michael: It won't be out of my hands, Stanley. Okay? I promise you that.

Stanley: Oh? Can you promise that?

Dwight: On his mother's grave!

Michael: No. No. Well, yeah. It is a promise. And, frankly, I'm a little bit insulted that you have to keep asking about it.

Stanley: It's just that we need to know.

Michael: I know. Uh, hold on a second, I think Pam wanted to say something. Pam? You had a look like you wanted to ask a question? Just then?

Pam: I was in the meeting with Jan, and she did say that it could be this branch that gets the ax.

Oscar: Are you sure about that?

Michael: Pam. Maybe you should stick to the ongoing confidentiality agreement of meetings.

Stanley: So you can't say for sure whether it will be us or them, can you?

Michael: No, No, No. No, Stanley. No. You did not see me in there with her. I said, "If Corporate wants to come in here and interfere, they're going to have to go through me." Right? You know, you can go mess with Josh's people [employees of the other branch], but I'm the head of this family, and you ain't gonna be messin' with my children.

Can you recognize the many knower behaviors in this scene? Michael refuses to be perceived as someone who doesn't know or may be wrong. He attempts to protect himself at all costs by using denial, bullying, giving false promises, and acting like a "tough guy." He is either hiding the facts or is in denial about his office's poor performance. He takes on an "us against them" mentality, even though the "them" is the same company he works for.

What Is a Knower?

In "Learning, Knowledge and Power," Fred Kofman defines a knower as "someone who obtains his self-esteem from appearing to be right." A knower is not willing to admit, "I don't know," and is not willing to be influenced. Knowers believe they know all that they need to know in order to address the situations that they're responsible for. They are not willing to be influenced, because being willing to consider what another person has to offer implies that they don't know all that they are expected to—an especially difficult admission for a knower to make.

Figure 3-1

Knower Decision Tree

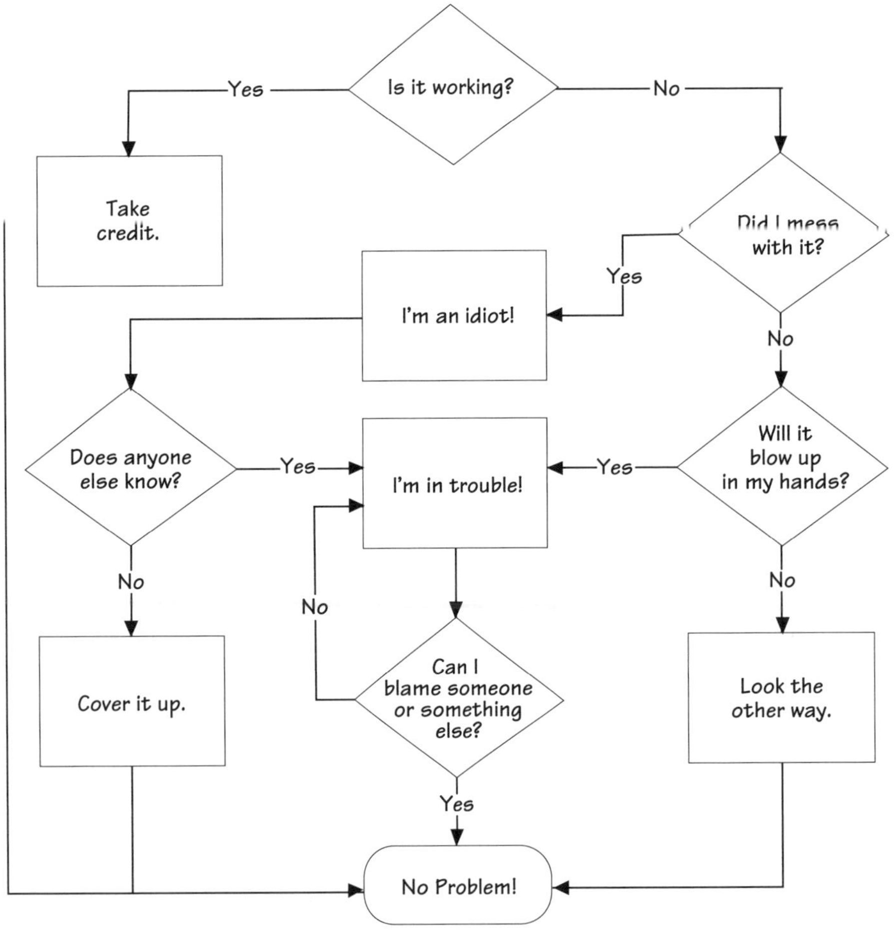

Knowing is so central to knowers' identities that it causes them to sometimes pretend that they know, even when they don't. But the role of a knower goes beyond an unwillingness to admit they don't know. They can easily admit to not knowing as long as it does not make them look bad. They don't care if they don't know about things that are unrelated to their personal competence and success.

Knowers can easily become defensive. For example, if they are expected to be responsible for addressing an area of poor performance, but they don't know what to do, they hide their lack of knowledge, blame someone or something else, conceal the evidence, ignore the situation, or deny that the performance was actually poor in the first place. Figure 3-1 offers a tongue-in-cheek illustration of this perspective.

What Is a Learner?

Learners are players in the game of life and understand they are there to have an impact on the game's outcome. Their primary and pervading value is one of unconditional responsibility (a term for which Fred Kofman has written an extensive description in *Conscious Business*). It's not that they blame themselves for all the ills in the world—that would be psychotic—it's just that they adhere to Peter Block's definition of responsibility (in *Stewardship: A Governance Strategy for the Learning Organization*): "To feel like whatever I am facing is my own." Because learners take this posture in relationship to reality, they see everything differently. Take note of how learners respond in these situations, as compared to knowers:

LEARNERS	KNOWERS
"Why didn't I bring my umbrella?"	"Why does it have to rain?"
"What caused me to react so defensively?"	"Why did they do that to me?"
"That's what can happen when I don't mark my lunch."	"Who ate my yogurt?"
"What do I keep doing that prevents me from leaving on time?"	"I'm really not that late, am I?"

When learners see themselves as players in the game, they put themselves in a position to address the problems they are facing, rather than blaming or sticking their head in the sand. The main focus of learners is on increasing their ability to respond to the challenges around and inside of them. They are willing to be influenced. They admit when they are uncertain. They consider what others have to offer.

Learners' security comes not from accomplishments, titles, or relationships, but from an inner knowing that they can face uncertainty with confidence. They are confident because they have a set of capacities for which they can reach whenever necessary to see connections, have conversations, or uncover aspirations that will illuminate and bring insight.

Learners have a rhythm to their life—a lot like breathing in and out . . . in and out. They become aware of reality and then choose a response . . . become aware, then choose. They retreat for reflection and then engage in action . . . reflection, then action. They suspend their assumptions and then get grounded in their beliefs . . . suspension, then grounding. They admit their ignorance and then offer their knowledge . . . admit, then offer.

This chart gives a quick overview of the differences between knowers and learners:

KNOWERS	LEARNERS
Publicly deny current results are less-than-desired when admitting so would make them responsible for addressing the discrepancy or would expose their lack of knowledge to improve the results.	**Publicly and unconditionally acknowledge current results are less-than-desired.**
Only publicly acknowledge current results are less-than-desired when the cause can be attributed to someone or something beyond their control or when doing so does not expose their current inability to improve the results.	**Publicly and unconditionally acknowledge current results are less-than-desired.**
Publicly deny responsibility for addressing less-than-desired results when they must also admit current inability to improve the results.	**Publicly accept unconditional responsibility for addressing less-than-desired results.**
Only publicly accept responsibility for addressing less-than-desired results when the cause can be attributed to someone or something beyond their control and when they deny inability to improve the results.	**Publicly accept unconditional responsibility for addressing less-than-desired results.**
Publicly refuse trying an alternative action strategy to achieve desired results and thereby hide their lack of knowledge to improve the results.	**Publicly acknowledge the need to try an alternative action strategy** and thereby admit their lack of knowledge to improve the results.
Always blame an external challenge to explain less-than-desired results.	**Always examine their "ability to respond" to explain less-than-desired results.**
Say they are competent and successful because they know.	**Say they know because they are competent and successful.**
Take action in order not to be *found out*.	**Take action in order to *find out*.**
Embrace certainty with insecurity.	**Embrace uncertainty with confidence.**

Having Knowledge and Being a Knower

Now, you might be thinking, "What's wrong with being a knower? Knowers possess valuable knowledge, don't they?" In fact, employers hire people for what they *know* to a great degree. Therefore, it seems that being a knower is actually a necessity for success, not a hindrance. Good point. Knowledge, or the ability to produce desired results through effective actions, *is* essential for being effective in the world. Having knowledge, however, is not the same thing as being a knower.

Knowledge in the hands of a knower is handled differently from knowledge in the hands of a learner. Knowers can use their knowledge very effectively within certain parameters—in situations that are static, definable, and understandable. For example, when a nurse discovers a patient in need of resuscitation, he assesses the situation within seconds and applies his current knowledge to that static, definable, knowable situation. He *knows* what to do in that situation, and acts skillfully and confidently. That kind of knowledge is a good thing, especially to the patient in that bed.

In other words, it is okay to be a knower but not to *stay* a knower. When current conditions change, or when unsatisfactory results are being produced (which happens frequently in today's world), knowers stop being effective. They react by applying the expertise they currently possess (the private, untested, or limited know-how that was useful for solving yesterday's problems) that may be mismatched for solving today's problems. Remember, a knower says, "I know all I need to know, and I am not willing to be influenced." In times of change, taking such a position, being unwilling to be influenced, and maintaining the same level of knowledge will make their knowledge obsolete. To paraphrase Eric Hoffer in *Reflections on the Human Condition*, "In times of change, learners will inherit the future, while the knowers will be perfectly equipped to live in a world that no longer exists."

In contrast, learners effectively apply their knowledge and expertise not by using autonomous, unilateral solutions, but by taking action to inquire further into the situation. Knowledge in the hands of a learner is understood as a part of the whole realm of insight surrounding a given situation and not the single, silver-bullet answer. Learners attempt to implement what they believe they know in order to find out whether they actually know it or not. When they see their own competence and success, they realize that they truly *know* something. Knowers think they are competent and successful *because* they know something.

Desired Results

Learning enhances your ability to produce desired results, and achieving desired results is the touchstone for everything contained in this book, so let's carefully define it. As Fred Kofman describes in *Conscious Business*, a result is made up of the interaction of two parts: a circumstance, change, or challenge, plus the ability to respond effectively to that challenge. For example, let's say the external challenge you are facing is your teenage son's rebellion against you. Because you fail to spend time with or engage him in meaningful conversation, your ability to respond is less than the challenge, and you will not achieve your desired results of a loving, trusting relationship with him. Alternatively, let's say your company is facing the external challenge of a recall of one of your products. You activate the rapid-response protocols you already have in place, and you make the most of your strong customer relationships. As a result of this effective ability to respond, you don't lose a single account, and you ultimately deepen your customer relationships.

A result, expressed in terms of equations, looks like this:

$$\text{Result} = \text{Ability to Respond} - \text{Challenge}$$

$$\text{Challenge} > \text{Ability to Respond} = \text{Negative Result}$$

$$\text{Challenge} < \text{Ability to Respond} = \text{Positive Result}$$

In other words, when your ability to respond exceeds the challenge that the world throws at you, you have learned, or achieved a positive desired result.

We often think of a challenge as something external, but that is not always the case. Our challenge could be something internal, like feeling an unusually high level of anxiety or fear. This fear could be driven by a perceived loss of something or someone. Even though this something or someone is an external entity, the feelings are internal. Likewise, you might be faced with a challenge in that you don't feel loved. That feeling is internal, and the party that neglects to do the loving is external. A challenge is a challenge, and a circumstance is a circumstance, whether internal or external.

Victim or Player?

The mentality of a knower can imperceptibly morph into a more insidious manifestation—a victim (the following discussion is based on Fred Kofman's explanation in "Learning, Knowledge and Power"). Interestingly enough, all learning must start with ignorance. To be a learner, you must admit ignorance. Those who are too afraid to acknowledge their ignorance feel trapped by their need to look competent, so they pretend to know, even when they don't. This pretending is central to the knower personality.

Pretending to know, however, puts knowers in a pickle. From time to time, they have to explain why they are not achieving desired results when they supposedly have all the answers. They have to justify recurring mistakes *without* taking any responsibility for them. This is tricky. So, knowers have developed a crafty escape hatch: They blame the external challenge (other people or circumstances) that is beyond their control. Remember, all results are the difference between one's ability to respond and the degree of external challenge. Because knowers are compelled to protect their ability to respond from all criticism, they will *always* choose the external challenge as the culprit. (Sometimes, knowers may admit that their inability to respond is the culprit, but then they will go on to blame *that* problem on some factor beyond their control.)

Another way to bring this point home is to make an analogy between knowers and learners, and victims and players. When you explain poor performance through factors beyond your control, you feel you are the victim of those circumstances. When you explain poor performance through your inability to respond to the challenge, you feel you are a player in your own life, not just a spectator. Knowers see themselves as victims of circumstances beyond their control. Victims always look at the "challenge" side of the equation to explain less-than-desired results. There is a severe consequence for this blaming mentality—knowers lose all their power. Since victims do not consider themselves part of the problem, they cannot see themselves as part of the solution either. As Fred Kofman says in *Consious Business*, "The price of innocence is powerlessness."

Learners, on the other hand, see themselves as players in their own lives. Players always look at the ability-to-respond side of the equation to explain less-than-desired results. They acknowledge the existence of factors beyond their control, but concentrate their attention on those factors they *can* influence. Learners see themselves as part of the problem, thereby giving themselves power to be part of the solution. One might say that the price for this type of power is taking responsibility.

Here are a few examples. A knower/victim says that a hospital is losing money because of reductions in federal reimbursements; a learner/player concedes it is because the hospital's ability to respond is sluggish and ineffective. A knower/victim says his high school team frequently loses because the athletic director scheduled them to play most of their games against difficult teams; the learner/player admits they are not playing together as a cohesive group. A knower/victim says she is an ineffective manager because she didn't receive the right training; a learner/player admits that her heart is really in working the shop floor rather than sitting in an office.

The terms *knower* and *victim* are not synonymous. Being a player rather than a victim—looking at one's ability to respond rather than at the challenge—is not sufficient for making a person a learner, but it is necessary. Likewise, *learner* and *player* do not mean the same thing. In addition to acknowledging unsatisfactory results and their inability to respond (as players do), learners must still be willing to take action—to try a strategy that is different from the one they have been using.

Non-Learners

In addition to knowers and learners, there is another category: non-learners. Non-learners are people who do not display the defensiveness of knowers and also choose not to learn. They do not base their self-esteem on how much they know, nor do they have a desire to achieve better results in a particular area.

This does not mean that non-learners are passive, sedentary, TV-watching slugs. They are just people for whom the issue at hand, whatever it is, is simply irrelevant. Or they might just feel ambivalent about it. You and I, from time to time, are non-learners, too. I am a non-learner when it comes to skateboarding, gardening, and ventriloquism, for example. I just don't care enough about those subjects to want to invest my time in learning how to perform them better. We each have thousands of non-learning areas in our lives. Non-learning is not usually a problem.

It can become a problem, though, if the area of non-learning is in a realm where you are expected to perform well, based on your role in life. If, for example, one of your duties in the family is managing the finances, but you are doing it poorly, your non-learning is a problem. It may not be a problem for you, because you are attaining your desired results—food is on the table, the kids are wearing clothes, you have a toothbrush, and so on. It is a problem for your spouse, however, when there is not enough money to afford a decent haircut or take a vacation. It's also a problem for the utility company, because they need to get paid for providing your house with electricity.

Non-learners facing the reality of not actually achieving their desired goals will necessarily transform themselves into either knowers or learners. The key word here is *desired* goals. If they do not truly desire better results, nothing will happen. But if they really do care about improving results, then either they will cover up the evidence, pretend that they really do know what they're doing, and blame external circumstances (like a knower); or they will admit that the situation has now become a problem and work on increasing their ability to manage the family finances (like a learner).

Am I a Knower?

Chances are pretty good that you have not adopted a knower stance to the same extent as Michael Scott in *The Office*. For one thing, he would never allow himself to be so humiliated as to read a book like this one. He might even create his own version and make us read it. So, the fact that you are reading this book means that you are willing to be influenced and therefore have an aptitude for becoming a learner. Even so, you may have recognized some of these knower tendencies in yourself and are asking yourself if you are indeed a knower. Don't worry too much about that question. Take some comfort in the fact that we are in this together. I admit I am a recovering knower. If you can admit your knower tendencies, then you are also a recovering knower. Only a recovering knower can become a learner. In the next chapter, we will explore this question a little further.

Rapid Recap

- A learner embraces uncertainty with confidence. A knower embraces certainty with insecurity.
- People are not learners until they (1) admit they are not currently achieving desired results, (2) admit that the less-than-desired results are theirs to address, and (3) admit that they need to try an alternative action strategy. They will also make these admissions to others (i.e., "go public").
- Having knowledge is not the same thing as being a knower.
- Achievement of desired results is the touchstone of every learning process.
- Results = Ability to Respond – Challenge
- When desired results are not achieved, knowers/victims blame this discrepancy on the challenge, while learners/players blame it on their inability to respond.

Reflective Response

- Think of a person you know who exhibits many of the characteristics of a knower.

    - When that person fails to achieve desired results, what do they blame—their inability to respond or the challenge they are facing?

- Think of a person you know who possesses several attributes of a learner.

    - When that individual is not achieving desired results, what do they blame—their inability to respond or the challenge they are facing?

- Are you a recovering knower?

Chapter 4

Are You a Knower or a Learner? A Self-Assessment

This chapter will walk you through five self-assessment activities to determine whether you tend to take either a knower stance or a learner stance. Previous chapters describe a knower in a less-than-desirable light, so you might feel some resistance to doing these activities because of what they may reveal about your thinking and behavior. This reluctance is natural and understandable, especially because we are all inclined to take a knower stance—that is how we are wired. But identifying this inclination is the first step toward growing beyond it.

If you think you have knower tendencies and anticipate these activities with some anxiety, let me offer words of advice. This may be hard to swallow, but that anxiety you are feeling is your knower inclination. The last thing a knower wants is to be exposed, so feel free to do these exercises in a secluded place. Also, realize that we are not 100-percent knower or 100-percent learner. We move back and forth between these states, depending on the issue. Try to think of the feedback from these activities as data, not as truth. Then you can use your findings as a basis for shifting your natural response.

Completing these activities is not the end of the story but rather the beginning. No matter what your answers reveal, the chapters ahead offer ways to use this information to move from a knower to a learner stance.

Let's go exploring!

Activity 1: Reactive Versus Creative Orientations

Steps

1. Make a list of the top 10 work issues that are important for you to address in the next two work days (essentially, your current to-do list):

_______________________________ ✓ ♥

_______________________________ ✓ ♥

_______________________________ ✓ ♥

_______________________________ ✓ ♥

______________________________	✓	♥
______________________________	✓	♥
______________________________	✓	♥
______________________________	✓	♥
______________________________	✓	♥
______________________________	✓	♥

2. Now, indicate the kind of energy that motivates you to address each of these issues. Ask yourself for each item, "Where does my energy or motivation to address this issue come from—*pressure* or *desire*?"
   a. Circle the ✓ (checkmark) next to the items where you are motivated *primarily* by a feeling of *pressure* to get them done; where you feel an external force or expectation that drives, or pushes, you to accomplish this item.
   b. Circle the ♥ (heart) next to the work issues where you are motivated *primarily* by a feeling of *desire* to achieve them; where some internal force, or passion, pulls you toward accomplishing this item.
3. Count the number of items that were motivated by pressure and the number of items motivated by desire, and write the numbers in the spaces below:
   a. Items motivated by pressure (no. of checkmarks circled): _____
   b. Items motivated by desire (no. of hearts circled): _____

Questions

1. Were more items motivated by pressure or by desire? Why?

2. Do the results of this activity surprise you or not?

Discussion

Individuals operate from two general orientations to make improvements in their world: the *reactive* (problem-solving) orientation and the *creative* orientation. (The concepts of "creative orientation," "reactive orientation," and "creative tension" were developed by Robert Fritz and articulated in *The Path of Least Resistance: Learning to Become the Creative Force in Your Own Life.*)

As illustrated in Figure 4-1, people who operate from the reactive orientation start by thinking about a problem, which causes them to feel pressure to solve that problem. As that pressure increases, it motivates them to take action to address the situation. Then what happens? The problem symptoms seem to go away. When the symptoms dissipate, the pressure to take action is reduced, and they don't feel any need to take further action and—guess what?—the problem symptoms come right back! Then the cycle starts all over again. The goal of a reactive orientation is to drive the problem pressure out of existence, but reactive problem-solving rarely ever works as a long-term solution. Knowers usually operate from a *reactive* orientation. They allow or expect external people or circumstances to define what their desired results ought to be.

Learners operate, to an increasing degree, from a *creative* orientation. It's not that they *never* react to their circumstances—it is often necessary that they do so. Learners, however, spend increasing amounts of their time working from a creative point of view, where they define their own results for themselves. They start by thinking about a vision they would like to achieve, which feeds their desire to bring that vision into existence. So, they begin to take action that would give them their desired result. Then what happens? They see progress toward their desired result, which further fuels their desire to achieve it, which motivates them even more to take action, which serves to spin this reinforcing cycle once again. The goal of this orientation is to bring something new into existence—namely, your desired result.

Figure 4-1

Reactive Versus Creative Orientation

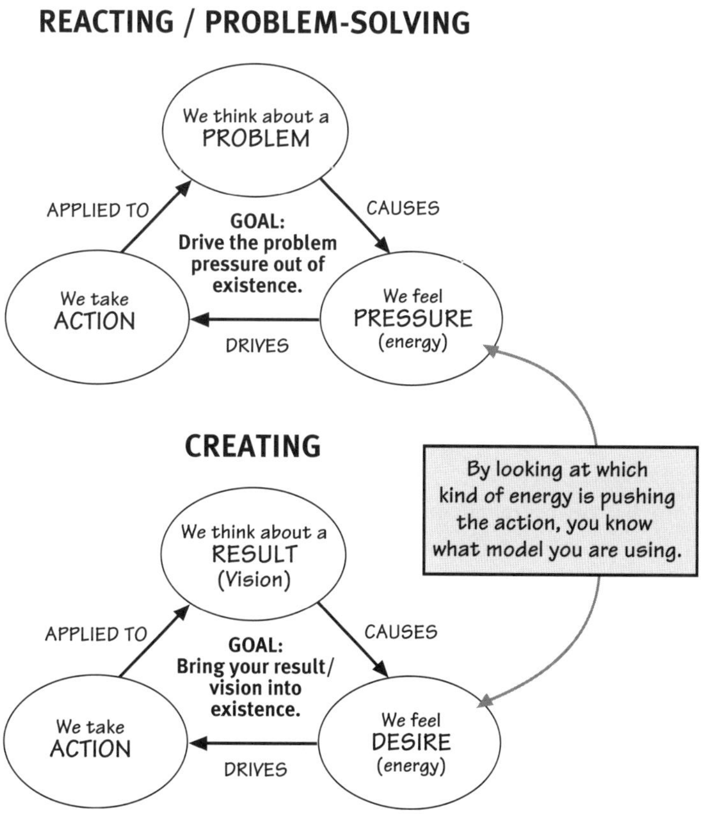
REACTING / PROBLEM-SOLVING
We think about a PROBLEM
CAUSES
We feel PRESSURE (energy)
DRIVES
We take ACTION
APPLIED TO
GOAL: Drive the problem pressure out of existence.
CREATING
We think about a RESULT (Vision)
CAUSES
We feel DESIRE (energy)
DRIVES
We take ACTION
APPLIED TO
GOAL: Bring your result/ vision into existence.
By looking at which kind of energy is pushing the action, you know what model you are using.

Activity 2: Compliance Versus Commitment Strategies

Steps

1. Think of a time when a change occurred in your life (at home or at work) that had a profound impact on you, *and* you were 100 percent *against* that change. List the change and the key factors that made you 100 percent *against* it:

   - *The Change:*

   - *Key Factors:*

2. Think of a time when a change occurred in your life (at home or at work) that had a profound impact on you, *and* you were 100 percent *in favor* of that change. List the change and the key factors that made you 100 percent *in favor* of it:

   - *The Change:*

   - *Key Factors:*

3. Look at your list of factors from Step 2. How many of them have something to do with one of these four statements below? ________

   a. You were acting on valid information, and all relevant information was shared with you.

   b. You could make a free, informed choice of the alternatives. You felt no pressure to accept one alternative over another.

   c. You felt that your personal vision and values were strongly aligned with the chosen direction.

   d. You had full participation in the discussions and decisions that led up to the change.

4. Describe a time when you had to convince one or more people to head in a direction that you were suggesting. From your point of view, it was imperative that they be strongly committed to this action, because this was a change that was to last a long time. List the actions you took to ensure your success.

   a. Look at the list of actions you just described. Put a checkmark in the box next to the items below that you paid a great deal of attention to while taking those actions:

      - ❑ You provided valid information and shared *all* relevant data, whether it would help or hinder your change effort. You didn't keep any information secret.
      - ❑ You encouraged a free and informed choice by those affected by the change. You did not sway them, and they felt *no pressure* whatsoever to choose one option over another.
      - ❑ You provided opportunities for the participants to share their personal vision and values, and to test whether the chosen direction was in alignment with *their* vision and values.
      - ❑ You included a majority, if not all, of those affected by the change effort in all the discussions and decisions throughout the change process.

Questions

1. Were more of the items you listed in Step 2 *related to* or *unrelated to* the statements listed in Step 3? Why?

2. How many boxes did you check in Step 4? Do you see a correlation between the number of boxes you checked and the long-term success of your change effort?

Discussion

We have all been a part of change efforts, either as the "changer" or the "changee." Think back to the groups you were a part of that made a significant shift. The leader likely used one of two general methods to get everyone operating from the same page: *compliance* or *commitment*.

Knowers operate from a *compliance* mentality. It is important for a knower to control as many factors as possible. So knowers who are leading a change effort will withhold certain information from others if it doesn't support their case. They will subtly, or not so subtly, make it known that there is a "right" way to go forward and a "wrong" way. They will also avoid allowing any expressions of whether the initiative falls in line with the vision and values of the participants, especially if they don't match the leader's vision and values. And finally, they will try to reduce the opportunities for those affected by the change to actually participate in the decision-making process. The leader might give token opportunities to react to the proposed direction but won't give full participative freedom.

Learners operate from the *commitment* mentality. Commitment to future direction, or desired future results, is developed through four practices: (1) generating valid information and sharing all relevant information, (2) allowing free, informed choice of the alternatives, (3) participating in discussions and decisions, and (4) aligning the chosen direction with personal vision and values. If any one of these elements is missing, then commitment to the suggested direction will not last.

Activity 3: Your Part Versus the Whole

Steps

1. Read the following article: ("Fights, weather reduce island's gray wolf population," *Muskegon Chronicle*, March 8, 2002, 6B)

> Deadly clashes between packs and unusually mild winter weather caused the gray wolf population on Isle Royale National Park to decrease from 19 to 17 over the past year, a scientist said.
>
> Only two years ago, 29 wolves lived on the Lake Superior island. But the animals seem healthy and the drop off is no cause for alarm, said Rolf Peterson, wildlife ecologist at Michigan Tech University in Houghton.
>
> While wolves decreased, the moose population rose from 900 to an estimated 1,100, said Peterson, who for 32 years has studied the predator-prey relationship between the two species on the island.
>
> "It's a lean year, but that's normal for wolves." Peterson said. "What evidence we have points to a food shortage."
>
> Peterson spends every January and February on the island and conducts most of his observations by air. He said that snowfall was the lightest he'd ever seen.

"Moose were in places where we don't normally see them in winter, on high ridges, in open areas instead of the conifer swamps," he said. Peterson says moose may face long-term problems because balsam fir trees, their primary food source, are dying off.

Because they could move around more than usual it was harder for wolves to attack them—even calves and older moose, which make the easiest targets.

Peterson said that his team observed numerous encounters between wolves and moose. That made the island's three packs more inclined to fight over the moose that were available. Nine of the 19 wolves that were alive a year ago had died—either in fights or from starvation.

On the positive side, seven pups were born—a sign of overall good health, Peterson said.

2. Based on this article, list the factors that affect the size of the wolf population.

3. Imagine you are Rolf Peterson, and you have decided to do something to increase the size of the wolf population on the island. Describe which factors listed above you would try to influence.

Questions

1. There are at least eight factors that have an affect on the wolf population (see Figure 4-2). How many of these did you list in Step 3? ________

Figure 4-2

Factors Affecting the Wolf Population

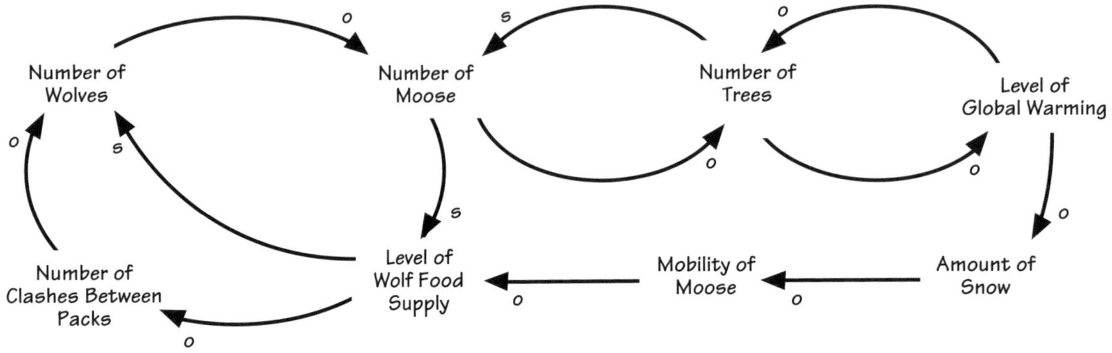

2. Did you happen to list global warming as a factor? Why or why not?

Discussion

This activity is intended to find out whether you are inclined to think in terms of your part or the whole. Knowers don't typically expand their list of factors that affect a problem beyond what is obvious. For this activity, most folks list "number of moose" and "number of wolf clashes" as the primary factors that affect the size of the wolf population. It is rare that they go beyond that. These factors are important, but they are short-term, near-sighted solutions. To think in terms of long-term, permanent answers, you would need to look elsewhere. The highest-leverage intervention, in this case, is to decrease the "mobility of the moose." Heavy winter snowfalls will naturally have this effect, but with global warming increasing, we can't count on that. So, as Rolf Peterson, you would have to devise another crafty method for limiting the mobility of the moose (snow-making machines, physical barriers, etc.).

Many of you probably didn't list "global warming" as a factor. Why? "Because it wasn't mentioned in the story," you might say. Someone operating from a learner stance would look beyond their own small realm (in this case, the words contained in the story) and ask questions that are not necessarily contained in the story, but are factors, nonetheless.

Knowers rarely take their focus off of their own realm, whether it is their job, task, team, department, family, and so on. Eventually, they will face a problem whose cause or effect lies outside of their domain. They will then become desperate and panicked (like *The Office*'s Michael Scott in Chapter 3), because they have not focused their attention on those outside factors. This dynamic drives them

Figure 4-3

Knower's Realm of Control

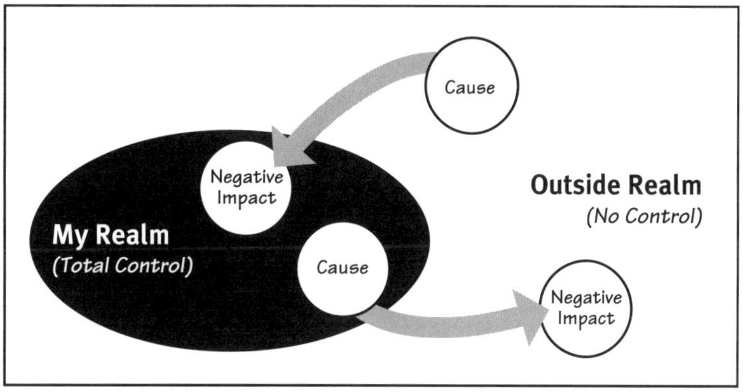

to protect themselves, or insist on their own way, or blame something or someone outside of their realm, without ever finding a solution to the problem.

Learners, on the other hand, often focus on factors or conditions *outside* their area of responsibility that influence factors inside their area of responsibility (see Figure 4-3). Instead of concentrating on who or what is causing the problem, they view problems as interconnections and influences in a broad web of relationships across boundaries. In a learner's reality, there is no such thing as factors being either inside or outside of anything. They are all just interrelationships in a huge system that has an effect on what they are trying to accomplish.

Activity 4: Protection Versus Reflection Modes

Steps

1. Think of a difficult, troublesome, or upsetting conversation you recently had. This should be an encounter that didn't go nearly as well as you would have hoped. It could be a situation in which you sensed that the other person didn't seem to get it or tense words were exchanged. Difficult conversations come in all shapes and sizes.

   Give a title to this difficult conversation:

2. Respond to the statements on the next page by indicating with a checkmark whether you "did" or "did not" do what the statement says, in relation to the difficult conversation cited above. *Do not respond to these statements as you think you* should *(a common tendency), but as you actually* did *respond in that situation.*
3. Compare your answers to those in the chart on page 43 to calculate your score. If your answer matched the "Best Response," then place a "1" in the "Your Score" column, otherwise, place a "0" in the column. Then, add your total score at the bottom of the "Your Score" column.

Statement	Yes, I Did	No, I Did Not
1. At some point along the way, I tried to avoid the conversation.		
2. I thought to myself "they probably are relying on information that I am not aware of."		
3. I tried to find out what needs or concerns the other person had that I didn't have.		
4. I felt like my line of thinking should be obvious to the other person.		
5. I thought that the problem at hand was their fault.		
6. I wondered how my actions, decisions, or comments affected the other person in a way other than what I intended.		
7. I found myself making "yes, but" statements in order to convince the other person.		
8. I assumed that if I provided enough evidence to support my position, the other person would see my point.		
9. I invited the other person to challenge my viewpoint or to point out information that I was missing.		
10. I felt that I had to "win" the disagreement in order for my ideas to be implemented.		
11. I thought the other person probably had good intentions and was just unaware of the impact they were having on me.		
12. I assumed that the other person's view was well thought-out and rational, just like mine.		
13. I thought it was essential to avoid an upsetting situation.		
14. I assumed the other person was strong enough to handle my concerns about their actions, decisions, or comments.		
15. I felt like I had the most accurate perspective on the problem at hand.		
16. I believed that the other person had bad intentions toward me.		
17. I asked questions about the other person's view in order to learn more about where they were coming from.		
18. I thought that the other person was ill prepared for the conversation or lacked sufficient knowledge about the problem at hand.		
19. I believed that the other person wanted to learn from their mistakes.		
20. I shared the thinking behind my position, including the data I noticed and my interpretation of that data.		

(The statements in the charts on pages 42–43 are adapted from Managing Difficult Conversations, *an interactive CD-ROM program by Chris Argyris, Peter M. Senge, and Bill Noonan; Harvard Business School Publishing, 2003. Used with permission.)*

Statement	Best Response	Your Score
1. At some point along the way, I tried to avoid the conversation.	No, I Did Not	
2. I thought to myself "they probably are relying on information that I am not aware of."	Yes, I Did	
3. I tried to find out what needs or concerns the other person had that I didn't have.	Yes, I Did	
4. I felt like my line of thinking should be obvious to the other person.	No, I Did Not	
5. I thought that the problem at hand was their fault.	No, I Did Not	
6. I wondered how my actions, decisions or comments impacted the other person in a way other than what I intended.	Yes, I Did	
7. I found myself making "yes, but" statements in order to convince the other person.	No, I Did Not	
8. I assumed that if I provided enough evidence to support my position, the other person would see my point.	No, I Did Not	
9. I invited the other person to challenge my viewpoint or to point out information that I was missing.	Yes, I Did	
10. I felt that I had to "win" the disagreement in order for my ideas to be implemented.	No, I Did Not	
11. I thought the other person probably had good intentions and was just unaware of the affect they were having on me.	Yes, I Did	
12. I assumed that the other person's view was well thought-out and rational, just like mine.	Yes, I Did	
13. I thought it was essential to avoid an upsetting situation.	No, I Did Not	
14. I assumed the other person was strong enough to handle my concerns about their actions, decisions, or comments.	Yes, I Did	
15. I felt like I had the most accurate perspective on the problem at hand.	No, I Did Not	
16. I believed that the other person had bad intentions toward me.	No, I Did Not	
17. I asked questions about the other person's view in order to learn more about where they were coming from.	Yes, I Did	
18. I thought that the other person was ill prepared for the conversation, or lacked sufficient knowledge about the problem at hand.	No, I Did Not	
19. I believed that the other person wanted to learn from their mistakes.	Yes, I Did	
20. I shared the thinking behind my position, including the data I noticed and my interpretation of that data.	Yes, I Did	

Your Total Score: ____________

4. Individuals who are operating from a knower stance will receive a low score on this quiz; those operating from a learner stance will score higher. So, someone who scored between 16 and 20 was attempting their conversation in "reflection mode," while someone who scored between 0 and 7 was having their conversation in "protection mode."

Questions

1. According to the quiz above, were you having your conversation more in protection mode or reflection mode? Does that surprise you?

2. If you had a low score on the quiz, how do you explain it?

3. In your answer to Question 2, did you explain your score by pointing to the other person or to circumstances (protection mode behaviors); or by looking inside and asking yourself, "I wonder why I acted like that" (reflection mode behaviors)?

Discussion

Knowers (and most all of us, actually) are predisposed to have difficult conversations in protection mode. Conversations become "difficult" when they concern issues that are threatening or embarrassing. And because we are not taught the skills to handle embarrassing or threatening situations, we are left to our own devises to protect ourselves. If you are in protection mode during a difficult conversation, you

- assume you are right.
- perceive yourself as more reasonable than others.
- assign negative attributes, intensions, and motives to others.
- see others as responsible for the problems.
- avoid upsetting situations.

Learners have developed the ability to participate in difficult conversations in reflection mode. You are in reflection mode during a difficult conversation when you

- accept you have only partial knowledge and the other party has relevant information too.
- assume they have a reasonable perspective, considering what they're up against.
- assume they are acting with integrity, given their situation.
- acknowledge you may be contributing to the problem.
- assume others want, and are strong enough, to learn from mistakes.

Activity 5: Deciding Versus Exploring Responses

Steps

1. Imagine you are a member of a group that is having a lively conversation. All the right people are in the room. The group has full authority and responsibility for making an important decision and is eager to do it. The exchanges below occur at some point in that conversation.
2. At the end of each of the three exchanges, think about what you would most naturally say next to complete the discussion. If you were actually in that situation, what would be the most typical move you would make? Write a sample of the words you would say in the space provided.

Exchange 1

You: Okay, let's start by talking about what we are going to do to improve our customer service performance. We have not yet achieved our goal, we have six months to go, and our numbers are basically flat.

Kyle: I think we have to do more of what we've been doing. I think we're making progress. Our numbers aren't rising as fast as we'd like, but they're not dropping either. We just have to be a little patient.

Tracy: So you think we can reach our goal by just doing the same thing?

Kyle: Yeah. It's not a very aggressive goal. We'll get there eventually.

Chris: You could be right. Maybe we're expecting too much too soon.

Pat: Four years ago, our actual scores were at the same level as this year's goal. Did you know that? It seems like we haven't made any progress since then. What does this tell us?

Jan: Yeah, but things are different now. The world has changed. We can't expect to get those same results in *this* environment.

Kyle: We've gotten complacent. We haven't focused our energies like we should have. We just have to rededicate ourselves to this goal. We've got to give it a higher profile.

You:

Exchange 2

You: Many options have been discussed and discarded so far, but Plan B seems to keep resurfacing and appears to be a favorite of the group. I feel comfortable going with Plan B. How do the rest of you feel?

Group Members: [Almost all of the group members express their support for Plan B.]

You: Chris, you've been kind of quiet. What do you think?

Chris: Well. I'm not sure. I don't exactly know whether I support Plan B or not.

Tracy: Why? What's the problem?

Chris: There's no problem. I'm just not sure about this plan. It seems like it's missing something.

Kyle: [To the group] Chris always drags his feet on everything. [To Chris] Why don't you make up your mind?

Jan: Look, he doesn't have to commit if he doesn't want to—we don't need consensus to move on, do we? I'm getting tired of this.

You:

Exchange 3

You: We've been talking a long time, and I just want to take a moment to review here. Are there any conclusions that you think we could make at this point?

Pat: We seemed to agree that Plan B was our highest leverage point, so I think we should invest 75 percent of our budget on Plan B and then meet next week to decide on how to spend the other 25 percent.

Chris: I think 75 percent is too much. We've got some other projects simmering on the back burner, and I'd like us to reserve more of our budget for them.

Sandy: Like what? Those so-called "back burner projects" haven't been discussed in months. Don't you think that if they were a higher priority we would have discussed them recently?

Jan: We did say that Plan B was our highest leverage point, so it makes sense to me that we spend at least 75 percent. But, why not spend 100 percent if we think it will get us where we want to end up.

Chris: Last month we said that Plan A was our highest leverage point and now were saying that Plan B is more important. So, we did talk about "back burner projects" recently.

Kyle: This is not the first time we have shifted our priorities this year. Our thinking just evolves. I don't want to go back and rehash that old Plan A stuff. Let's go with plan B, and I say 75 percent is fine.

You:

3. Let's divide your responses into two categories: (a) those that had the intention of continuing or resolving a debated topic, or closing down options; or (b) those that had the intention of uncovering or creating emerging new insights through mutual learning, or opening up the options. The first type of response we will call "deciding responses"; the second type we will call "exploring responses." Look at your three responses.
    a. How many of your responses were deciding responses? ________
    b. How many of your responses were exploring responses? ________

Questions

Did you give more deciding responses or more exploring responses? Why?

Discussion

Individuals who take a knower stance typically guide group discussion using *deciding* responses; someone working from a learner stance typically guides group conversation using *exploring* responses. This does not mean that deciding responses are wrong—they are perfectly viable moves to make; they just serve a different purpose than exploring responses. The deciding responses help move the group toward problem-solving and narrow the options until the supposedly best one is selected (appropriate when that is the purpose of the conversation). The exploring responses help move the group toward not-yet-considered ideas and open up opportunities for deeper learning and, perhaps, later consideration.

This activity is useful for distinguishing between a knower response and a learner response. Knowers will tirelessly focus on debating what is known, while learners concentrate some of their attention on delving deeper into what new insights might emerge. Knowers never comment on the mental framework the group seems to be operating under; unlike learners, who point out and question this mental framework or thinking (i.e., "Do you feel we are really clear about what we think will work to achieve this goal?").

Using This Experience

Now that you've gone through these activities, you can say that you have had some firsthand interaction with these knower and learner behaviors (within the limits of a book format). At a minimum, you should have a little more insight into the distinction between the two kinds of behaviors and where you might fall along the knower-learner continuum. Chapter 7 will revisit some of these experiences as we tie them into overcoming the secrets of a knower with concepts and tools from the five learning disciplines.

You are probably unaware of it, but there is an underlying set of thinking habits that affected the way you went through these last exercises. The next several chapters will address the structures that provoke and hold these knower/learner behaviors in place. They will also reveal the thinking habits that predispose us to behave like knowers from time to time, and then suggest what we might do to change those patterns of behavior.

Rapid Recap

- The characteristics and behaviors that learners share are that they
  - operate from a creative orientation (not reactive orientation).
  - act out of a commitment mentality.
  - view problems as interconnections and influences.
  - conduct difficult conversations in reflection mode.
  - guide group discussion using exploring responses.

Reflective Response

- As a result of experiencing these activities, how would you characterize yourself: a knower, a recovering knower, or a learner?

Chapter 5
The Learner's Path

Some things in life are true, no matter what you think of them, or so powerful that you really can't change them. For example, the law of gravity cannot be changed—it just is, so we must adjust to it. As we discussed earlier, the increasing pace and persistence of change is another phenomenon that has become a dominant reality in our lives, and we must learn to navigate it successfully. The *Learner's Path*—a conceptual framework that describes the underlying process of learning—has similar qualities. You cannot change this process of learning—you must learn to align with it.

The Learner's Path is not a prescriptive model; it simply describes the decisions people necessarily make—often subconsciously— when they set out to achieve their desired results (or when they learn). This underlying process (shown in Figure 5-1) consists of a series of five questions that individuals (or a group of people) successfully answer as they increase and expand their learning. A "successful answer" isn't always a "yes" and isn't usually the answer we would prefer to give. It is, however, an answer that aligns with the learning process.

Figure 5-1

The Five Questions

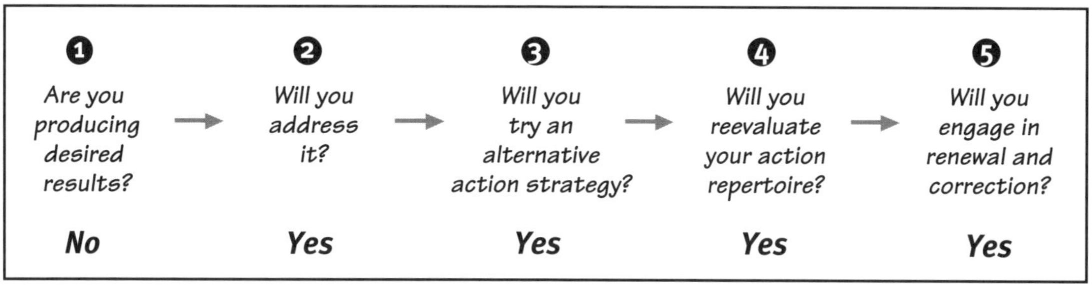

1
Are you producing desired results?
No
2
Will you address it?
Yes
3
Will you try an alternative action strategy?
Yes
4
Will you reevaluate your action repertoire?
Yes
5
Will you engage in renewal and correction?
Yes

Awakeners

In order for learning to begin, individuals need to snap out of the non-learner posture. They need to become aware of any discrepancy between their desired result and their actual result. In other words, they have to *wake up*. Two kinds of "awakeners" can lead someone to take the first step on the Learner's Path (see Figure 5-2):

- *A desire to create a new life or a new result.* This awakener rouses the person from the inside-out. Spiritual practices and personal passions can play a role here, as well as structured activities that facilitate a growing desire to create something new, such as guided imagery, prayer, and mission statements.
- *Feedback that contradicts their belief about the results they thought they were getting.* This is an outside-in awakener. Some information from the outside startles the person into recognizing that the results they are getting are not as good as they should be. Sometimes this feedback comes in the form of consequences because of actions or inactions (i.e., disgruntled staff, marital troubles). Sometimes it comes in the form of a volatile environment (i.e., a dynamic new competitor enters the industry, gasoline prices soar).

Whatever rouses them, this is the moment when an individual wakes up, starts paying attention to their actual results, and chooses either a knower or a learner stance. As fellow travelers on the Learner's Path, we can facilitate one another's learning by gently providing awakening feedback to one another, as appropriate.

Figure 5-2

Awakeners Leading to the Learner's Path

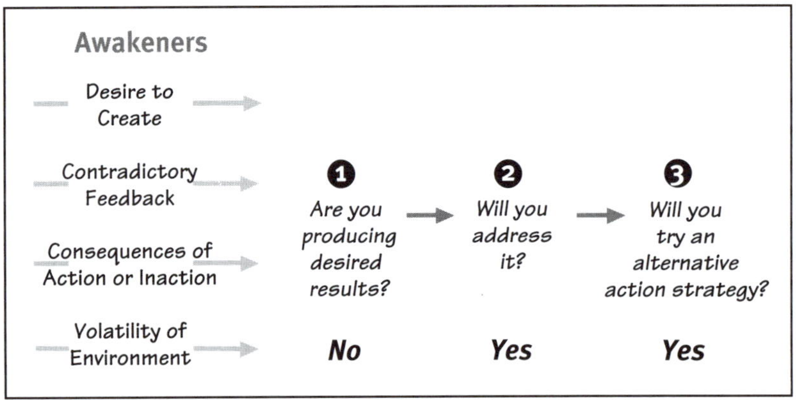

The Three Critical Learner's Path Questions

The essential, underlying distinction between knowers and learners is the way they answer the first three questions of the Learner's Path. Learners will successfully answer all of these questions and even publicly disclose their answers; knowers get stuck on one or more of the questions, and when they do, they never reveal this information publicly to anyone else. Let's look at these three questions in turn.

QUESTION 1: ARE YOU PRODUCING DESIRED RESULTS?

Learning always starts by becoming conscious of a discrepancy between "the way things are" and "the way things ought to be." If the first question is answered with a "no," then learners admit to some dissatisfaction with the status quo. They want something more or better. They recognize a gap between what they have and what they want, between who they are and whom they would like to be, or between what they seem to be creating and what they would like to create. If someone is completely content with what they have, who they are, or their present circumstances, then there is no impetus whatsoever to begin learning. Knowers may or may not admit that they are dissatisfied with their current reality, but learners are clear on this point.

Not everyone agrees that having dissatisfaction with current reality is a necessary ingredient for learning—it sounds so negative, doesn't it? You might be thinking, "What about being totally satisfied with current reality and still being curious about something in addition—isn't that good enough to be a learner?" I would have to agree with you—it *is* good enough. And, I would add that curiosity, or an aroused interest to gain an additional or new understanding of something, suggests some dissatisfaction with one's current level of information about that "something." The first distinction between knowers and learners, then, is that learners *always* admit that they are not producing desired results—they want something more or better.

I want to add one important caveat. This framework does not differentiate between a "good" desire (e.g., helping people in need, becoming healthier, getting along better with your relatives) and a "bad" desire (e.g., exploiting or hurting yourself or others). The source of, and motivation for, your desired results matters greatly, but I will have to leave it to another book, because it is beyond the reach of this one.

QUESTION 2: WILL YOU ADDRESS IT?

Learners who answer this second question positively are willing to take some responsibility for addressing the gap between the way things are and the way they want them to be. This does not necessarily mean that they accept blame for those less-than-desired results. It means that they see some connection between themselves and their results, are willing to own part of the situation, and are resolved to take some action to address it.

For example, say a manager feels that his boss is the only one who could do something about improving outcomes in their department; the manager doesn't feel he has the proper authority to make any changes. In other words, he is saying that the issue isn't his to address. By shifting perspective, however, the manager can begin to understand that he *can* choose to take some responsibility for addressing the situation after all—he can have a conversation with his boss. As simplistic as that sounds, this is a breakthrough of sorts for the manager. He is taking a step toward learning rather than blaming.

Sometimes knowers *may* actually admit that they are not achieving desired results, but then they go on to make excuses, blame others, or complain about unreasonable expectations. If they care at all about improving desired results, but they are not willing to take any responsibility for making changes, they are left with the miserable plight of merely wishing that someone else will do something to improve the results. Knowers, therefore, feel no impetus to pursue learning; they think that someone or something else should deal with the less-than-desired results, if it is even needed.

I am part of a neighborhood association of about 25 homeowners who occasionally meet to do business of mutual concern. The first meeting of the association was peppered with accusations, raised voices, misunderstandings, blaming, posturing, talking over one another, and confusion. From my perspective as a professional organizational development facilitator, I thought the meeting was fascinating. I work at a fairly evolved organization, so I rarely see such dysfunction in a group. Memories of group facilitation and productive conversation techniques came flooding back to me. "I can *do* something about this mess," I said to myself.

It was clear to me (as I internally answered Question 1) that we were not achieving desired results. No one left the meeting feeling as though it had been productive. I wasn't sure I wanted to keep attending these gatherings unless somebody did something to make them more constructive. However, when I began to entertain Question 2, "Will I address it?" my heart sank a little. "Me? Why should I have to address it? I'm not the one behaving badly! The chairman should do a better job of controlling the meeting. And it will take so much work, anyway. I really don't have the time to spend on this problem." I created a whole list of excuses for why it was not my issue to address. So, even though I answered Question 1 successfully, I did not do so with Question 2. Unless I was willing to take some responsibility for dealing with the issue (whether through coaching people, giving private feedback, tutoring the chairman, or offering to facilitate the meeting), it was impossible for me to become a learner in this instance.

The second distinction between knowers and learners, then, is that learners will *always* acknowledge that improving the less-than-satisfactory results is their issue to address.

QUESTION 3: WILL YOU TRY AN ALTERNATIVE ACTION STRATEGY?

Remember the discussion from Chapter 3 about choosing whom or what you would like to change—yourself or someone/something else? Question 3 asks you to try an alternative action strategy, but if you have already decided that someone/something else must change rather than yourself, then you really are not learning. So you need to be careful at this point to make sure that you have decided that it is *you* who needs to change, and then you can decide to try an alternative approach.

Figure 5-3, an expansion of what was shown in Chapter 1, gives you a more complete understanding of what happens after you decide that you need to change. You will choose one of thee levels of change: change your *doing* (Question 3 provokes this choice), change your *thinking* (Question 4 provokes this choice), or change your *being* (Question 5 provokes this choice).

By answering the third question in the affirmative, learners acknowledge that they must begin to use a different action strategy than they are currently employing if they want to achieve their desired results. They have come to a realization that if they keep using the same old approach, they will just keep getting the same old outcomes. Essentially, they are admitting that their current action strategy is not effective. This is especially hard for knowers, because their self-esteem depends on knowing "how," and if they have to change their action strategy, they are also admitting that they don't really have the necessary knowledge. If a person isn't willing to try something different, there will be no learning, because learning requires new action.

Figure 5-3

Expanded Stance Decision Tree

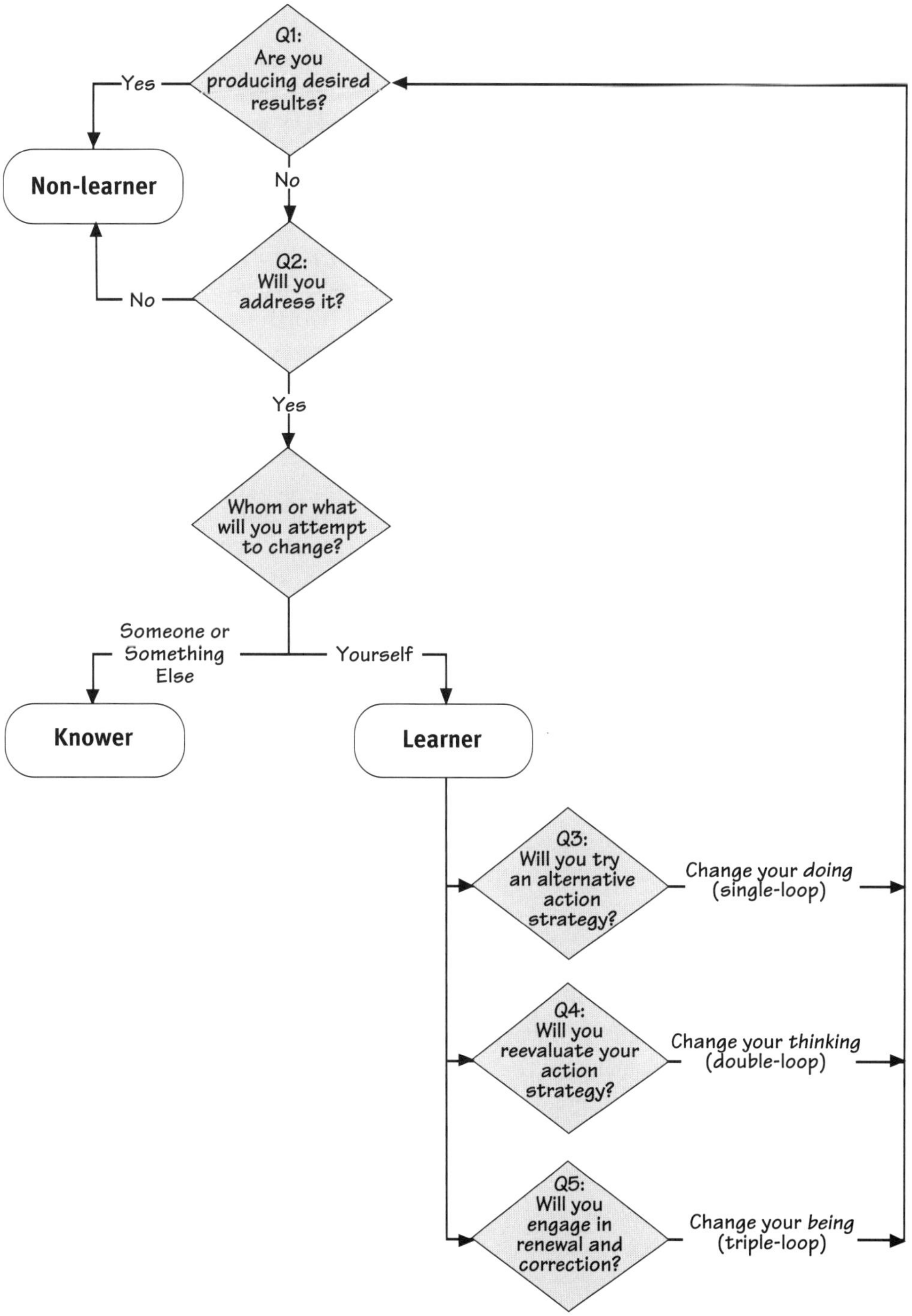

When I was in college, I worked as an industrial janitor at a manufacturing plant. After being there for more than a year, I felt it was time for a raise. I mentioned this desire to my immediate supervisor, Jim, and he said he would talk to Don, my boss's boss, to make the arrangements. After the raise did not appear in my next paycheck, I wondered whether I should talk to him again or just wait another pay cycle. I did not want to get on his bad side, because I really, really needed the job (and a raise, of course). I decided to wait another cycle and was disappointed again when my pay remained the same. So, I decided to talk to him a second time and eased into a conversation about my raise. "Oh yeah—don't worry," he assured me, "Your paperwork must have gotten mixed up or something." So I waited another pay cycle, and guess what? No raise.

This was getting annoying, so I went to talk to him again. This time, he alluded to something about budget constraints and overhead and other concepts I had no clue about. I got the sense that things were not looking good, but he hadn't said "no" yet. One day, I left a note in his office and then tried to stop him on the factory floor for a moment to ask him if he had seen it. As he walked on, he yelled over his shoulder, "Yeah, yeah, I saw it, and I think [whatever, whatever]. . . ." I had no idea what he had said, so I resigned myself to my minimum wage job.

Then, one day, I got a sudden insight that I should bypass Jim and talk directly to Don. I knew this was risky and wasn't sure I had the guts to even attempt it. My opportunity came one day when Jim was in Don's office having a conversation. I sidled up like a cop about to burst through a door. As soon as I saw Jim open the door to leave, I pounced. As my heart pounded and my ears turned red, I asked Jim if he wouldn't mind coming back into Don's office, because I had a question I wanted to ask both of them.

What was the insight that spurred me to take new action? First of all, I recognized that I was not achieving my desired result (I hadn't gotten my long overdue raise). Second, I was willing to address this situation (in fact, I had attempted to address it several times). So far, so good. I then had to wrestle with the third question: Was I willing to try an alternative action strategy? Dealing with Jim wasn't working. I knew that if I kept doing what I was doing, I would just keep getting the same results. Did I have the courage to try another approach? This is one of the central issues to address when faced with the third question. By the way, the risk paid off. I got a whopping 10-cent raise, and I kept my job—at least for a little while.

So, the third distinction between knowers and learners is that learners will *always* admit that it is necessary to use an alternative action strategy in order to achieve desired results.

Knowers will get hung up at any one of these three decisions: Either they insist that current results are just fine (when they're *not*); they expect someone else to do something about the poor results (when they *should*); or they think their current action strategy will work just fine (when it won't). Something in the thinking habits of knowers keeps them stuck in one of these three places—a phenomenon we will discuss in greater detail in Chapter 6.

More Questions for Deeper Learning

Only the first three questions of the Learner's Path have been described. When learners answer these questions successfully, they are engaging in single-loop learning—they change their *doing*. Learners use questions four and five to explore deeper and higher-leverage learning opportunities (see Figure 5-4). Knowers are left long behind at this point.

Figure 5-4

The Learner's Path

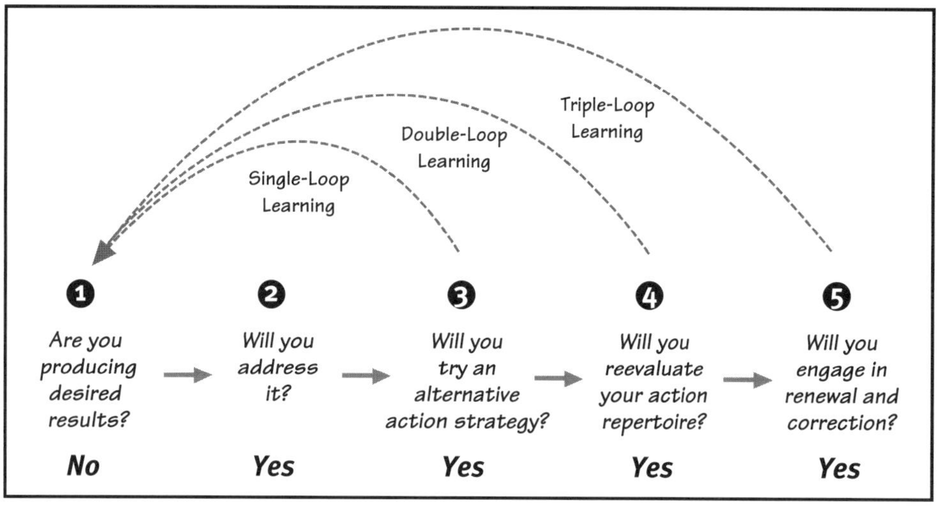
Single-Loop Learning
Double-Loop Learning
Triple-Loop Learning
1 Are you producing desired results? No
2 Will you address it? Yes
3 Will you try an alternative action strategy? Yes
4 Will you reevaluate your action repertoire? Yes
5 Will you engage in renewal and correction? Yes

QUESTION 4: WILL YOU REEVALUATE YOUR ACTION REPERTOIRE?

When learners have cycled through the first three questions several times (admitting less-than-desired results, taking ownership for addressing the issue, and trying some alternative approaches) and are *still* not achieving desired results, then they seek to answer the fourth question. Here, they admit that they must use an action strategy that is beyond their action repertoire (the stock of strategies they can reliably employ to achieve desired results), and they move into double-loop learning—they change their *thinking*. At this level, they expand their action repertoire through questioning their assumptions and replacing those that are obsolete.

During my freshman year in college, I roomed with my best friend from high school. We were inseparable during high school and the summer before our freshman year. We had developed habits of relating to one another that worked in high school but were causing strain in our relationship during college. For years, Matt had been, in my eyes at least, my protégé. I always felt somehow responsible for looking out for him. During our freshman year, he started hanging out with new friends (how dare he!) and asserting more and more independence from me (after all I had done for him!). This adjustment to a relationship between equals, rather than a subordinate-superior relationship, was hard for me to accept, so I tried to "keep him down" whenever I could. This, of course, only escalated things, because he resented my imposing anything on him, and he ramped up his efforts to break free of my dominance. Our friendship survived until the end of the year, but by then we spent quite a bit of time apart.

We really never talked about what happened; we each had our own version. He got married, I finished school, and we saw each other only occasionally. But when we had matured enough, we talked about why we were unable to get along during college. In an "aha!" moment of awareness, I understood that my limited action repertoire at that time enabled me to get along with Matt only if I perceived him to be my subordinate. I did not know how to relate to him in any other way.

From that conversation on, even though I wasn't aware of it at the time, I engaged in double-loop learning. I challenged and replaced my assumptions about what it took to relate effectively to Matt. We talked in new ways, about new things, and in new places. Even though our respective family commitments prevent us from seeing much of each other these days, I still consider him one of my best friends and think of our relationship as one that definitely benefited from double-loop learning.

QUESTION 5: WILL YOU ENGAGE IN RENEWAL AND CORRECTION?

If learners have cycled through the first four questions several times and are *still* not achieving their goals, they need to move on to the fifth question: Are you ready to look closely at yourself and engage in personal renewal and correction? This is triple-loop learning—changing your *being*. In triple-loop learning, learners further expand their action repertoires through deep self-assessment, and replace obsolete understanding of their self-concept and current abilities.

After college, before getting married and starting a family, I was quite active in a number of competitive sports. It was a big part of who I was. I would commute a hundred miles, twice a week, to play on a recreational basketball team, for example. I also played softball on a coed team.

I would frequently get frustrated with the players on my team because we were losing every game. I felt as though I was doing my part, hitting home runs, playing shortstop, and so on. But we were making too many mistakes, and we had a lot of weak hitters. Some of our players did not even completely understand the rules. It was about all I could stand.

One woman on our team was a standout, though. Karen could field and hit like no one else—she was probably the best woman in the whole league. I would watch her hit home runs, field flawlessly, and then proceed to throw angry fits when one of our teammates would make a mistake. She rolled her eyes when one of our weaker players came up to bat and yelled at teammates who threw the ball to the wrong base.

In many ways, Karen and I were kindred spirits. There were times when I fantasized about the team we could make if we could just replace some of these players. But then I had an epiphany. As I watched her get incensed once again during a game, I realized I was looking at myself—and I didn't like what I was seeing. My self-esteem was so wrapped up in winning that I forgot who I really was.

This realization is the essence of the fifth question: In order to achieve your desired results, you will need to replace obsolete understandings of your self-concept. That day, I decided to kill my win-at-all-costs competitive nature. I realized it was getting in the way of what I wanted in my life—contentment. Over the years, I learned to enjoy other elements of sports besides the win/loss record: the people, the setting, what happens before and after the games, and so on. For many years, we rarely won any games (Karen had moved on), but we occasionally won the league sportsmanship award. I had discovered a whole new way of being.

Learners don't necessarily always go from single- to double- to triple-loop learning in succession. Some learners (often those who are tackling deep, spiritual, or personal development issues) move directly into triple-loop learning without going through the other levels. Double-loop learning, however, *does* require a learner to progress through the single-loop process, because double-loop learning double-loops *on*, and tests the assumptions *of*, previous single-loop actions.

Rapid Recap

- The Learner's Path describes the underlying process of learning—steps you *must* go through to learn.
- When people successfully answer each of the first three questions of the Learner's Path and are willing to make their answers public, they have become learners.
- Knowers are unable to successfully answer one or more of these first three questions and will avoid revealing this fact to anyone else.
- When people answer the first three questions successfully, they are engaging in single-loop learning.
- When people answer the fourth question successfully, they are engaging in double-loop learning.
- When people answer the fifth question successfully, they are engaging in triple-loop learning.

Reflective Response

- Recall a time when you increased your ability to achieve desired results in some area of your life (in other words, you learned something). Give this new ability a label.

  ____

- Now, review the steps or stages you went through in this process and answer the following questions:
  - Did you admit that you weren't achieving desired results—that you wanted something more or better? [Question 1]

    Did you tell anyone about this?

    ____

  - Did you choose to become responsible for addressing (at least part of) this area of less-than-desired results? [Question 2]

    Did you tell anyone about this?

    ____

  - Did you decide that it was time to start using a new action strategy because the old one didn't seem to work anymore? [Question 3]

    Did you tell anyone about this?

    ____

- If you chose an issue that required particularly deep learning, try reflecting on the following questions as well:
  - Having reached the end of all that you knew how to do, did you admit that your previous strategies were no longer working and that it was time to reevaluate your action repertoire? [Question 4]

    Did you tell anyone about this?

    ____

  - Did you recognize that there was something about your self-concept or your habitual approach that prevented you from achieving your desired results and that it was time to engage in renewal and correction? [Question 5]

    Did you tell anyone about this?

    ____

Chapter 6

How Knowers Get Stuck: The Secrets of a Knower

In Chapter 3, we looked at the fact that knowers need to save face and appear knowledgeable (even when they are not), because their self-esteem depends on being right and sure. The dominant reality of knowers is the constant need to defend and/or protect themselves. What are they defensive about? What are they protecting themselves from? From being exposed as *not* knowing. There are times, however, when knowers will admit to *themselves* that (1) they're not achieving desired results, (2) it's their issue to address, and (3) it's time to use a different action strategy, but they just can't admit these things to *anyone else.* This is precisely what distinguishes learners from knowers. Learners can go public with successful answers to all of these three questions; knowers can't.

Figure 6-1

Where Knowers Get Stuck

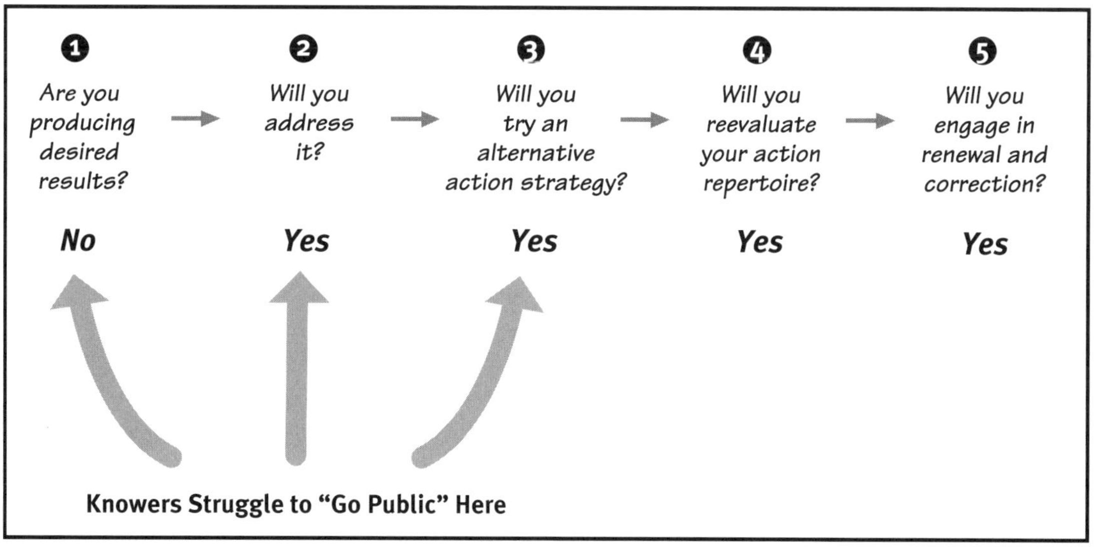

1 Are you producing desired results?
2 Will you address it?
3 Will you try an alternative action strategy?
4 Will you reevaluate your action repertoire?
5 Will you engage in renewal and correction?
No
Yes
Yes
Yes
Yes
Knowers Struggle to "Go Public" Here

Knowers' need for self-esteem-by-knowing can be traced back to a set of five thinking habits that protect their ego but have devastating effects on achieving their goals. When this set of thinking habits collides with the first three questions of the Learner's Path, knowers behave defensively, protectively—in other words, get stuck. And when they get stuck, they look for the escape hatch: explaining the circumstances, rather than examining their own inability to respond.

The Thinking Habits of a Knower

By the very act of answering the Learner's Path questions, you are creating behavior. And by looking at your behavior, then, we can infer your thinking habits and thus your openness to learning. Typical knower responses to the first three questions of the Learner's Path are explored below. The secret thinking habits that prompt knowers to give these answers follow directly.

THINKING HABIT 1: REACTING

Question 1 of the Learner's Path asks, "Are you producing desired results?" Learners will always say "no" to this question. They always want to achieve something more or better than what they currently have. Here are some of the predictable responses from knowers (or non-learners) when they are confronted with Question 1:

- I don't know what I want.
- I don't really care if I am producing desired results or not.
- My results are fine—compared to other people's results.
- To be honest, I'm just pretending that I *am* achieving desired results.
- All I know are the results I *don't* want to see—what I want to get rid of.

The first thinking habit of knowers is their belief that *other people and circumstances define what their desired results ought to be*, so they must constantly react. Answers such as "I don't know what I want," "My results are fine compared to other people's results," and "All I know are the results I don't want to see" all indicate that knowers believe they are at the mercy of other people or circumstances to define their desired outcomes. They perceive themselves as victims of things beyond their influence. They also think that the necessary approach to improvement is to constantly eliminate the problem symptoms that bombard them, which keeps them perpetually running on a problem-solving treadmill.

THINKING HABIT 2: COMPLIANCE

The second thinking habit, which applies particularly to group settings, is that *the leader forces group members to comply with his or her way in order to get things done*—manipulating the members of the group to see things the same way the leader sees them. This thinking habit is based on the assumption that groups work most effectively when they are in alignment (most of us would agree with this assumption). And because Thinking Habit 1 states that desired results are defined by someone or something outside ourselves, knowers have to devise a way to get group alignment while addressing volatile environmental factors. So they force compliance on the group. Knowers, as leaders, cannot allow the members of the group to have significant input into the definition of desired results because (1) it would violate Thinking Habit 1, and (2) it would bring them into unknown and untried territory, an intolerable situation for a knower.

There is one more thing to notice here. Responses to Question 1 do not all have to fit in the categories of knower or learner. A perfectly appropriate response, usually given by non-learners, is "I don't really care." They are ambivalent about the issue or they see it as irrelevant. It is impossible to care about everything.

THINKING HABIT 3: MY PART

The second Learner's Path question asks, "Will you address the less-than-desired results?" Learners will always answer this question with a "yes." They believe that they are responsible for addressing some aspect of the situation that has created the less-than-desired results. Knowers would predictably respond with the following answers when confronted with Question 2:

- I don't have enough authority to address it.
- It's not part of my job, therefore it's not my problem.
- It's too big of a responsibility for me to handle.
- I didn't make the mess, so I shouldn't have to clean it up.

The third thinking habit of knowers is that *they focus exclusively on their own little piece of the world.* This habit clearly determines the responses given to Question 2. All four responses relate to knowers' definition of "their part" or "their realm." The reason knowers say that the issue isn't theirs to address is because, in their view, the authority, the problem, the responsibility, and the blame all lie outside their domain.

THINKING HABIT 4: PROTECTION

When Learners answer Question 3, "Will you try an alternative action strategy?" they will always say "yes." They recognize that the action strategies they have been using are ineffective and that they need to try something different. We can predict how knowers would typically respond to Question 3:

- I just don't know what to do next.
- The pain of changing is greater than the pain of staying the same.

This thinking habit is a belief that *we must protect ourselves during conversations.* It has a lot to do with getting beyond (or, more accurately, *not* getting beyond) our usual views of the world. When knowers say, "I just don't know what to do next," what they are really saying is, "Considering my little perspective, from my little world, I have reached the end of all that I already know how to do, and I won't engage anyone else to get ideas because that would make me look like I don't know what I'm doing." When knowers engage in a conversation with someone about what to do differently to achieve desired results, they will steer the discussion away from themselves to safe topics that diffuse the fact that previous action strategies didn't work and that this happened on "their watch," or in "their realm."

The second typical response comes from the same seed as the first. When the "pain of changing is greater than the pain of stating the same," a knower will choose the pain that is known—staying the same. Again, because knowers do not expose themselves to alternative perspectives (they are too busy protecting themselves), they really have no one with whom to explore this "pain of changing." Maybe the pain of changing is not as great as previously thought because someone else has made this change before. But by protecting, rather than reflecting, knowers will never find out. Now, all they are left with is their own perceptions, within which they are trapped.

THINKING HABIT 5: DEBATE

The fifth thinking habit of knowers is that *they direct and debate during group interactions.* This thinking habit, like the previous one, relates to not getting beyond our usual views of the world. Because we know that knowers will have conversations in protection mode (Habit 4), it makes sense that they will not open up their view to alternatives. The result is that they remain desperately stuck with "not knowing what to do" and avoiding the "pain of change."

The Behavior Habits of a Knower

As demonstrated above, knowers' thinking habits have a profound impact on their behavior. Now we will explore a little further the kind of thoughts and actions these thinking habits actually produce.

1. **Knowers let other people and circumstances define desired results for them.** As a result of this perspective, their life is dominated by solving problems. That is how they are effective and make progress. The energy they feel every day comes from opportunities to immediately apply "what they know" against a definable, existing situation. They are stuck in this problem-solving orientation because it is the only orientation that allows them to stay within the realm of the "knowable." They feel a sense of control and are protected from seeing, in themselves, any possible shortcomings. But the problems knowers solve are really just an attempt to eliminate the symptoms they are experiencing rather than any effort to create long-term, fundamental solutions. They resist creating fundamental solutions to problems because doing so would (a) require them to design something that does not yet exist, thereby admitting that they don't have the whole picture, and (b) eliminate the best source of their "effectiveness" in the world—problems!!—and why would they want to do that?
2. **Knowers force groups to comply with their way to get things done.** They know that groups work together better when they all operate from the same page. Therefore, when they work on a team, they seek to convince others that they have the "right page" and all the others have to do is follow them. If someone suggests alternatives, knowers will try to shut them down or point out problems with their ideas, because they might be headed into untried territory—an area that is just too threatening. If knowers are part of a group in which they have authority, they will try to manipulate the members through rewards, punishments, policies, memos, procedures, and so on to instill a culture of compliance.

3. **Knowers focus exclusively on their own little piece of the world.** Because their aim is to control things as much as possible and to make things around them predictable, they focus almost exclusively on their team, their department, their group, their family, and so on. And the more variables they can gather into their sphere of influence, the better chance they have of controlling them. If they can make sure that their areas of responsibility perform well, then they can blame areas outside their realm when problems occur. Knowers must also keep the internal workings of their area a secret in order to ensure that they can do things their way. They do not like others trying to suggest how their work could be done better. They resist interacting with outside entities unless they can get something from them that will make their area function better. Even if a suggested change would benefit the organization as a whole, they are very resistant to suboptimizing anything from their area. They do things their way in their area. Period.
4. **Knowers protect themselves during conversations.** Their objective in every conversation is to "win." If they can be seen as "right," as "rational," and as "not-responsible for problems," they have successfully protected their image as a competent person. Because their self-image is dependent upon appearing competent, any conversation that points out that they may not have all the information, may be illogical, or may have contributed to a problem must be stopped. Knowers use secret conversational strategies that counter-attack such threats. They attempt, at all costs, to defend their beliefs and conclusions, because a chink in their paradigm armor could cause extraordinary stress for them. It would threaten the core beliefs upon which they base all their "knowing."
5. **Knowers direct and debate during group interactions.** They expect group members to interact by playing out predictable, consistent roles, which they reinforce by directing the interaction and controlling the agenda as much as possible. If they can put people in a little box, then they can better control the process and predict the outcome of their conversations. They constantly bring up what worked for them in the past, as a way of maintaining the focus of attention on areas where they have expertise. They use their position power to intimidate or subtly manipulate the conversation, so that the outcomes are in line with what they want. Knowers often work out the details of a plan in advance and then present it "for approval." When someone challenges their plan, knowers make the others prove why their approach is better than theirs. Giving up control, acting as a peer with people who report to them, and leaving silence and space for spontaneous insights is seen as pure foolishness.

Let's revisit Michael Scott's meeting with his coworkers in *The Office* (from Chapter 3), where he perfectly demonstrated the five thinking habits of a knower.

- He focused only on his own little "realm," protecting and controlling as many functions and people as possible, and he pit "his" office up against the other branch and against corporate headquarters.
- Most of his conversations were designed to protect himself or his point of view. Considering another's point of view was not even on his radar screen.
- He forced subordinates to comply with the norms that he was trying to establish, like "ongoing confidentiality agreements."

- He used other people and outside circumstances to define what his desired results ought to be. He was exclusively acting out of a reactive orientation, constantly putting out fires, and applying quick fixes, as if he were on a problem-solving treadmill.
- He directed and debated during group interactions, controlling the agenda and other people.

The Secrets of a Knower

As you can see from this discussion of thinking habits, these are not topics knowers are particularly proud of or would want to discuss in public. That is why I call them "the secrets of a knower." For example, a knower would never say, "By the way Jack, my habit is to think only in terms of my own little piece of the world, so I won't be taking any responsibility for improving results today." Nor would she say, "Hey, Sara—I just wanted you and the other team members to know that I'm in the habit of making you comply with my way, so I won't need any of your input during this meeting." These thinking habits are well-protected secrets.

Now, if some of this discussion is hitting a little close to home and you are seeing yourself in these descriptions, you might be feeling a little uneasy. In some ways, what we've covered up to this point in the book may appear to be an elaborate effort to set a "knower trap"—multiple things coming together to back you into a corner. Being a recovering knower myself, I have empathy for what you may be feeling.

First of all, I painted a contrasting picture of learners as the "good guys" and knowers as the "bad guys." Then I introduced the Learner's Path, and because it is the underlying process of learning, it forces us to answer particular questions, thereby revealing behaviors that knowers would prefer to keep covered up. Third, I showed how those knower behaviors (typical answers to the questions) can be used to infer knowers' ingrained thinking habits, which reveal that knowers are predisposed to focus on anything but themselves. And finally, I unceremoniously slammed the door on their escape hatch—which is to blame their lack of effectiveness on the external challenges. This, seemingly, leaves knowers with no way out. What is a knower to do!?!

The best way to spring this trap is to change our thinking habits. If we could shift our thinking habits, then we would be more willing to look at ourselves and engage in developing our ability to respond to the challenges that assault us every day. And if we are willing to change ourselves, then we'll be living, increasingly, from the learner stance. Our answers to the Learner's Path questions would become routine rather than threatening. And our ability to achieve desired result would grow mightily.

So that is where we will next set our sights—overcoming the secrets of a knower. As we continue this journey, our objective is not to immediately destroy these thinking habits but instead to replace them with more effective ones. We'll delve into that process in the next chapter.

Rapid Recap

- By observing a person's behavior in answering the Learner's Path questions, we can infer their thinking habits.
    - Knowers have five particular thinking habits that prevent them from successfully answering the Learner's Path questions.
- Uncovering one's thinking habits is the first step to changing them and, thereby, opening up to learning.

Reflective Response

- Which one of the five thinking habits of a knower hits especially close to home for you?
    - Why do you think that is?

Chapter 7

Overcoming the Secrets of a Knower

[**Author's Note:** *If, in reading earlier sections of this book, you realize that you possess knower tendencies, then this chapter is for you. If you've concluded that you are indeed a learner, then proceed to Chapter 9 for information to challenge and guide you deeper into the learning process.*]

You *can* overcome the "secrets of a knower," as described in the last chapter. The diagram below illustrates the movement that I believe every person can make from knower to learner by applying the five disciplines of organizational learning (as described in *The Fifth Discipline*). They are:

- **Personal Mastery:** developing personal effectiveness and the ability to create the results we most desire
- **Shared Vision:** creating collective aspiration and mutual commitment
- **Systems Thinking:** understanding the whole, and how structures and systems are interconnected
- **Mental Models:** reflecting on our attitudes and perceptions to increase mutual understanding and insight into ourselves
- **Team Learning:** generating collective insight by transforming how we think and interact

Figure 7-1

Moving from Knower to Learner

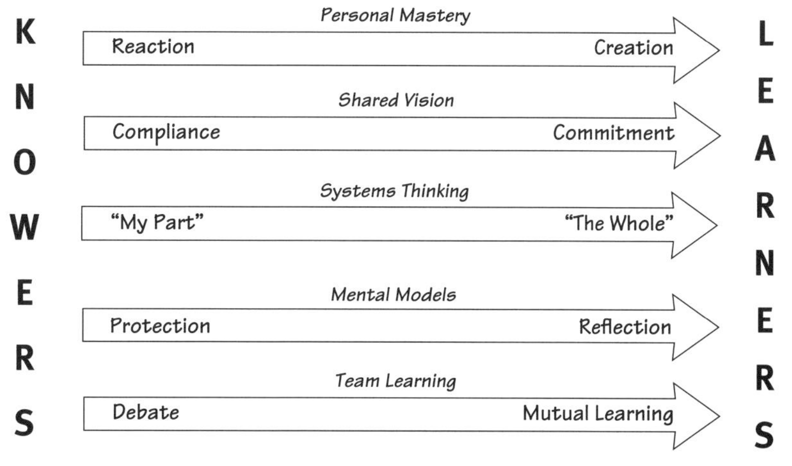

A New Application of the Five Disciplines

When I first started working in a "learning organization" (that is, an organization where people seek to learn rather than know), I didn't entirely understand what that term meant. I believed that if we practiced the five learning disciplines, we would somehow, together, build a better organization. I operated under the assumption that if I, or another top leader, merely said organizational learning was a good idea, then my fellow leaders would adopt it as well. I also assumed that these leaders possessed a high level of maturity, introspection, and desire for self-development.

In several instances, this was true. For the leaders who were on fire to engage in self-development and effective leadership, these learning practices served to fuel the flames with tools, techniques, and frameworks that made everything seem like, in the words of our CEO, "God-given common sense." I assumed for years that everyone was on an accelerated self-development path, all due to the practice of these five disciplines.

The truth surprised me. The majority of the leaders who had participated in training sessions, who had enjoyed a pleasant and challenging experience, and who had agreed that the organizational learning concepts were helpful ideas, then returned to their work responsibilities without ever using them. This was a startling and troubling realization. For years, these leaders had failed to practice the disciplines on a regular basis, and I hadn't detected that lapse. My hypothesis—that teaching them *about* the learning disciplines would transform them into progressive and effective leaders—was destroyed.

It became my quest to understand why some leaders consistently practiced the disciplines, even when others, equally exposed to the same training, failed to do so. I discovered that there was a difference in the way they answered certain questions (which later became known as the Learner's Path). Essentially, the first group were learners and the second group were more like knowers. But how did they get that way? How did the progressive leaders get to the point of being receptive to the learning disciplines, and how did the less-than-progressive leaders become resistant to them? What would I need to do to prepare both groups for the real work of applying the disciplines? Would I have to abandon the effort if the person attempting to learn them was not predisposed to do so? Or could the disciplines themselves prepare one to apply them in a more advanced way later on?

In pursuing the answers to these questions, I discovered that progressive leaders/learners weren't the only ones who benefited from practicing the learning disciplines. Even the less-than-progressive leaders could use them as tools to *become* learners. In short, I discovered a new and different application of the five disciplines.

From Knower to Learner with the Five Disciplines

Notice that these concepts are called "the five disciplines," not "the five tips" or "the five good ideas." They are not steps, habits, lessons, points, insights, or rules. They are called *disciplines* for a good reason: Learning them entails training and practice. You cannot develop your ability to practice a discipline by attending a six-hour workshop, reading a book, or going on a weekend retreat. You become proficient only by systematically and persistently practicing them over many years.

Does "over many years" sound like too much? Consider this comparison: How long would it take you to become proficient at a sport such as golf or tennis? Years, right? The same thing is true for learning the five disciplines. The more time you dedicate to practicing them, the faster you will become good at them. And think about this comparison, too: How long did it take you to develop your knower habits, and how long have you been practicing *them*? In the Introduction, I mentioned that my knowing started at an early age and that it took more than 25 years to perfect it. I will not become a true, full-blown learner overnight. In fact, I have been on my intentional journey from knower to learner for more than nine years, and I'm still making progress—so, you, too, can expect to make steady improvement over time.

The following sections build on the experience you had with the activities in Chapter 4 and will suggest how you can overcome some of the secret knower tendencies you may have discovered there. You will be directed to some selective tools or methodologies, under the umbrella of the five disciplines, along with descriptions of how to use them. This is a brief synopsis of deep and well-developed practices, tools, concepts, and models. To get a full explanation of the learning disciplines, refer to Peter Senge's *The Fifth Discipline* and *The Fifth Discipline Fieldbook.*

From Reaction to Creation

Activity 1 in Chapter 4 (page 33) gave you a glimpse of the difference between living from a reactive orientation versus living from a creative orientation. You saw that, when operating from a creative orientation, desire energizes you to pursue better results; and when you're operating from a reactive orientation, pressure becomes the source of your energy. If you think of your life as a car, then living from a creative orientation is like driving the car, and living from a reactive orientation is like being the passenger—you're just along for the ride. If you behave exclusively out of reaction to events or challenges, life seems like a continuous series of problems (created and defined by others) to solve—as if you are living on a problem-solving treadmill. It feels as though you are continually playing a role rather than living from your heart. Before long, you will wonder what happened to the *real* you. Knowers get stuck in a reactive orientation because one of their secrets is to let other people and circumstances define their desired results.

When knowers are confronted with the first question of the Learner's Path, "Are you achieving desired results?" they will often get stuck because all they know of desired results is a desire to get this current pressing problem "out of my face."

Recovering knowers have to unplug the treadmill for a moment and give deep consideration to what they want in their lives or what they want to do *with* their lives. So the discipline of personal mastery will help them define their aspirations for themselves, and shared vision will help them do so collectively.

PERSONAL MASTERY

I decided to start defining my own desired results and stop relying on others to define them for me. I found the motivation to do so by listening to an appeal from my spirit: "Do you really want to strangle me just so that you can protect your self-esteem and persona?" Heeding this internal call for something deeper and more profound, I began to draft a mission and vision for my life. Using various books and techniques over a year, I generated a personal mission that felt comfortable and that I revisit from time to time to tweak or confirm. This mission has become a foundation for pursuing my creative orientation.

Some straightforward resources I have seen used effectively for generating a personal mission statement include *The Path*, by Laurie Beth Jones; *The 7 Habits of Highly Effective People* and *First Things First*, by Stephen Covey; and *What Color Is Your Parachute?* and *How To Find Your Mission In Life* by Richard Nelson Bolles.

Even though I had embraced this novel way of being, I had no idea how to live more from the creative orientation. It is difficult for knowers to bring something new into existence when their sense of worth is based on knowing what *is*. The act of creating, by necessity, means that I do not and cannot know all about this thing that does not yet exist.

Figure 7-2

Creative Tension Model

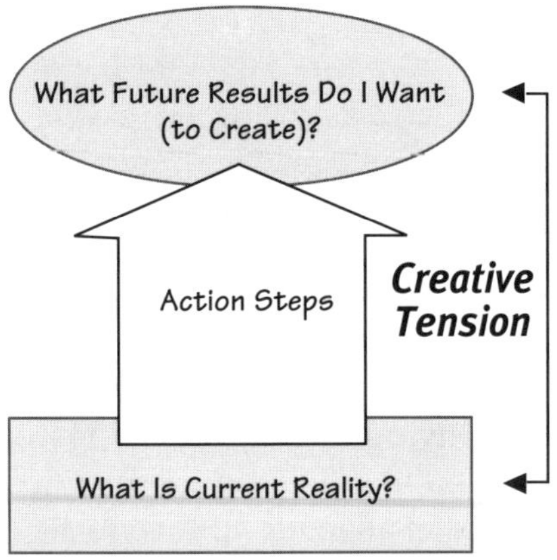

The big idea that helped me take a step in the right direction was Robert Fritz's "creative tension model." The creative tension framework gives structure to the ethereal idea of bringing something new into existence (introduced as the "creative orientation" in Chapter 4). It juxtaposes an honest and accurate awareness of current reality with a precise mental picture of your vision, or what you want to create. I have to admit, though, that I still feel some anxiety about pursuing something that is not-yet-created. But defining a precise mental picture of future results certainly helps recovering knowers to reduce their anxiety about the unknowable, uncontrollable future.

In addition, knowers can have a hard time looking at current reality when the results of their efforts are inadequate and they have had some responsibility for achieving them. The practice of creative tension helped me see these unsatisfactory outcomes in a broader context. Now, I see less-than-desired results as just part of a larger, three-part scheme of success. Action steps, current reality, and my vision are all part of one thing (see Figure 7-2). Within the creative tension model, unsuccessful actions are not *mistakes* but *new learning*, which then become part of the new current reality. Therefore, even if my existing state falls short of my goals, I can apply what I've learned from my unsuccessful actions to developing a new strategy for achieving my vision.

So, to overcome the secret habit of letting other people and circumstances define our desired results for us, we need to define our own goals by living from a creative orientation. The creative tension model offers a broad and useful scheme of success.

From Compliance to Commitment

Your experience completing Activity 2 in Chapter 4 (page 36) should have helped you recognize the difference between doing something out of compliance (with someone else's external expectation of you) and doing something because of your internal commitment to that cause. Perhaps you glimpsed the dedication, alignment, engagement, or the focus you felt when you were 100-percent committed to a given action or direction. Or, alternatively, you may have remembered the resentment, apathy, or helplessness you felt when you were expected to be compliant. This activity may have made you also realize that you try to convince others to head in your suggested direction by using compliance tactics rather than commitment tactics. Why do we tend to act this way in group settings? Because the second secret of a knower—that we must force group members to comply with our way—motivates us to manipulate the members of the group to see things the same way we do.

SHARED VISION

To overcome the secret tendency to try to get others to comply, practice the discipline of shared vision. The goal of shared vision is to seek group alignment by using a long-term commitment strategy rather than a short-term compliance strategy. To a knower, a shared vision means "I have a vision, which I will now share with you"; but the problem is, these "visions" don't stick, aren't powerful, and aren't necessarily shared among the members of the group.

When I was leading a hospital group called the Education Council, I would prepare each month (in advance and in secret) a new version of the plan for hospital-wide education. Between meetings, I would study and "improve" our plan with technical innovations that the group had never heard of. Then I would make the group discuss the merits of my new plan and ways to implement it. With polite compliance, the members of the group followed along for many months. It was not apparent to me that my efforts were failing and that the compliance was turning into passive-aggressive resistance. In a moment of clarity, I later realized what I was doing and humbly acknowledged my role in wasting our time. We regrouped to discover a new vision, shared by all group members, that yielded an innovative patient treatment pathway that is still being used several years later.

The compliance strategy for group alignment can work, but only for a short while. Eventually, people will rebel, resist, sabotage, or leave. Why? Because their commitment to a future direction has to be cultivated through four practices:

1. generating valid information and sharing all relevant data;
2. allowing free, informed choice of the alternatives;

3. encouraging participation in the discussions and decisions; and
4. aligning the chosen direction with personal vision and values.

If any one of these elements is missing, then commitment to the suggested direction will not last. In the case of the Education Council, the members started to feel manipulated, their trust was diminished, and their commitment to the decisions we made plummeted.

Moving from compliance to commitment strategies is a difficult transition for knowers to make. I had to move from having control *over* others to having control *with* them. Knowers don't operate from a shared control mentality. Breaking down the commitment strategy into four elements, however, is tangible and comforting for a knower. All of these practices are designed to spread control among the members of the group rather than maintain it in my hands alone. In addition, giving weight to other people's ideas instead of insisting on my own actually has a counterintuitive effect. The more I include their ideas, the more they appreciate and respect me. And when it is time for me to share my thoughts (as part of comparing many proposals), my perspective could well carry more weight, without my having to insist on it. In the end, I may have to sacrifice short-term comfort and compliance, but I gain long-term commitment and momentum. The reciprocal trust that the discipline of shared vision produced made me much more willing to consider being influenced in the future.

Overcoming the second secret of a knower requires that you commit to co-creating the four conditions for shared vision. By learning these practices, you will feel aligned with your coworkers, build trust with one another, and create a sense of mutual commitment toward a shared future. The actual techniques for creating these conditions are the same ones used in the disciplines of mental models and team learning, which will be discussed below.

From My Part to the Whole

Have you ever played the pencil-and-paper game called "9 Dots"? The challenge is to connect the nine dots by drawing four straight lines without lifting your pencil. Most people draw their lines within the imaginary box implied by the eight dots on the border. The only way to solve this puzzle is, literally, to get "out of the box" and make three of the lines go beyond the implied border of the dots (solution on page 88, Figure 7-4).

Figure 7-3

The Nine Dots Puzzle

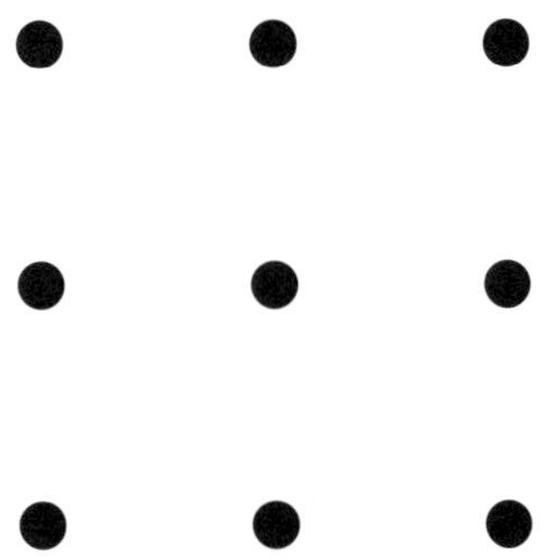

You may have found that your response to Step 2 in Activity 3 (page 39) stayed within the implied borders of the wolf and moose story (that is, the words printed in the story). If you have had this experience in other contexts, did you frame the problem you were trying to solve with self-imposed, imaginary "borders," and did you became stuck, not knowing what to do next? I have been caught in this trap of focusing on "my part" rather than on "the whole" many times. As knowers, we get caught here because our secret thinking habit is to focus solely on our own little piece of the world. I focus on my part because it is knowable, controllable, and containable, and it fits in nicely with my ability to address problems. I also have a quick and easy way to blame others when the problem is not in "my area."

So far, you may be thinking that the "my part" thinking isn't such a bad deal—where's the down side? Basically, there will come a point where "my part" cannot be successful unless I can interact with "the whole." I will no longer be able to claim my lack of contribution to issues and still be seen as effective.

SYSTEMS THINKING

The way to overcome the secret of focusing exclusively on my own little piece of the world is to apply the practices of systems thinking. After much study of systems thinking, I encountered these dilemmas:

1. What if the effect of a problem outside my area was creating a problem within my area, and the cause of the problem was not contained in my sphere of control? As I pride myself on solving problems and knowing all about my domain, I had better be able to fix this kind of problem. But because I have focused exclusively on my area, I really don't know how to go about addressing it in areas other than my own. Should I admit that I don't actually know all about my area after all, or do I admit I really can't solve this problem?
2. What if something within my part was the cause of a problem for someone else outside of my realm? It is unbelievably embarrassing to have to admit to "outside people" that my area isn't as good as it could be.

So, when a cause or an effect of a problem falls outside of my area, it appears that I cannot be both the expert in how to run my area and the problem-solver extraordinaire (see Figure 4-3). I found that the solution to this dilemma was to look *wider*, broadening the scope of what I pay attention to beyond my little piece of the world; and to look *deeper*, examining factors hidden below the surface. When I finally embraced looking at the world through the systems thinking lens, my effectiveness grew significantly. As Virginia Anderson and Lauren Johnson write in *Systems Thinking Basics*, "It becomes clear that everything is dynamic, complex, and interdependent. Put another way: Things change all the time, life is messy, and everything is connected." In a world like this, a knower's struggle to understand and maintain control becomes a desperate one.

If knowers are feeling stuck at this point, it is usually because they are hesitant to face the second Learner's Path question, "Will you address it?" They're not willing to address it because they believe it's not part of their realm of responsibility or because they didn't cause it. The next two sections will help them to reconsider that position. If they are willing to look wider or deeper, they may just discover a leverage point that can help them be more effective.

LOOK WIDER

One aspect of systems thinking that appeals to a knower is that it helps decrease the "unawareness" of the factors that influence the problems I am facing in my area. I can now know the factors that are removed from me in time and space (that occur after a delay and/or take place somewhere else). Tools such as "causal loop diagrams" (a sample of which is used to describe the wolf and moose dynamics in Chapter 4) helped me see problems as part of a broader web of interconnections and influences (even across departments), rather than as just "my screw up" or "their problem."

Causal loop diagrams can be used simply by beginners and with great complexity by advanced users. I'll give some rudimentary tips here, and if you want to dig deeper, you can visit Pegasus Communication's web site (www.pegasuscom.com) for multiple resources. A helpful way to think of causal loops is as "what causes what loops." The causal loops "work" by using arrows to depict how one variable has an impact on another, causing the target of the arrow to either increase or decline. The arrows are either designated with an "s" (a change in the *same* direction) or an "o" (a change in the *opposite* direction). In the portion of the wolf and moose loops reproduced in Figure 7-5, you can see how one variable affects another. For example, an arrow connects the number of wolves to the number of moose. The arrow has an "o" on it, so it shows that, as the number of wolves increases, the number of moose decreases, or moves in the *opposite* direction. Or, we can see that when the number of moose increases, the wolf food supply changes in the *same* direction, also increasing (designated with an "s" arrow). Pretty simple, really.

Figure 7-5

Sample Causal Loop

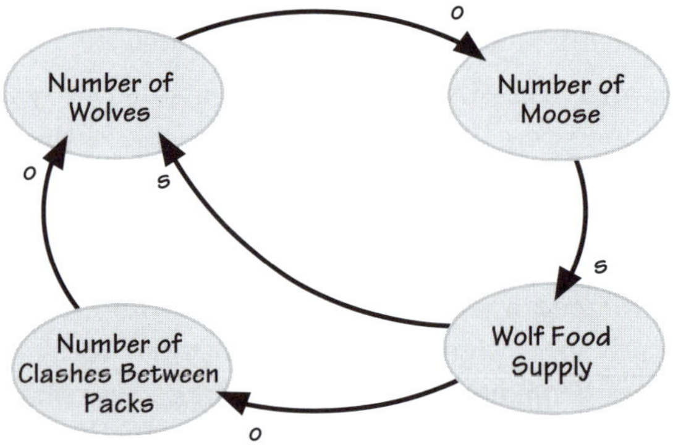

The simplicity may be deceptive, though, because it is completely dependent on defining the variables with great care. The arrows communicate a change in the level of something, so the variables have to be able to vary over time (strengthen or weaken, increase or decrease). You should use nouns, not verbs ("swimmers," not "go swimming"). You should be able to define a level of this variable (e.g. number of . . . ; strength of . . . ; quality of . . .). And be careful not to define the variables as events (e.g. mixed the paint; applied the paint; watched the paint dry). Process maps are better tools for showing the "first this, then that" nature of events.

In addition to causal loops, two simple tools have been helpful for assisting recovering knowers to see a problem no longer as "out there," but as something to which they are interconnected and on which they have an influence. Creating "Doom Loops" (so-called by Jennifer Kemeny—with a sense of light-hearted irony, I trust—in a workshop at a *Systems Thinking in Action®* Conference) helps recovering knowers identify a closed loop of feedback around a specific problem issue. When this is done successfully, there can be a profound "Aha!" moment as the participants in the exercise realize they, or other parts of their organization, are "actually doing this to ourselves." This will open up high-leverage options to take action.

Figure 7-6

Doom Loop Template

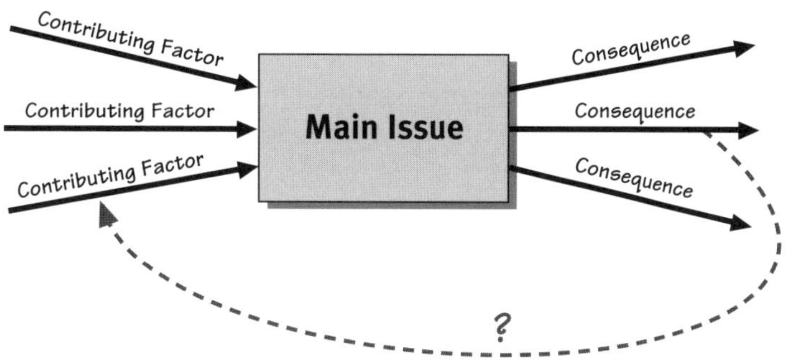

Participants create Doom Loops by first writing the main issue to be addressed (usually a problem) in the middle of the page. Then they brainstorm three main contributing factors that seem to sustain the existence of this problem issue. Next, they brainstorm three main factors that seem to be consequences of the existence of this problem. Finally, participants thoughtfully consider if any consequences feed back to any of the contributing factors, to create a closed, self-reinforcing loop. The question mark in the diagram indicates a place to add an additional factor that would help make a connection between consequences and contributing factors. (See Figure 7-7 for an example of a completed Doom Loop.)

Figure 7-7

Doom Loop Example

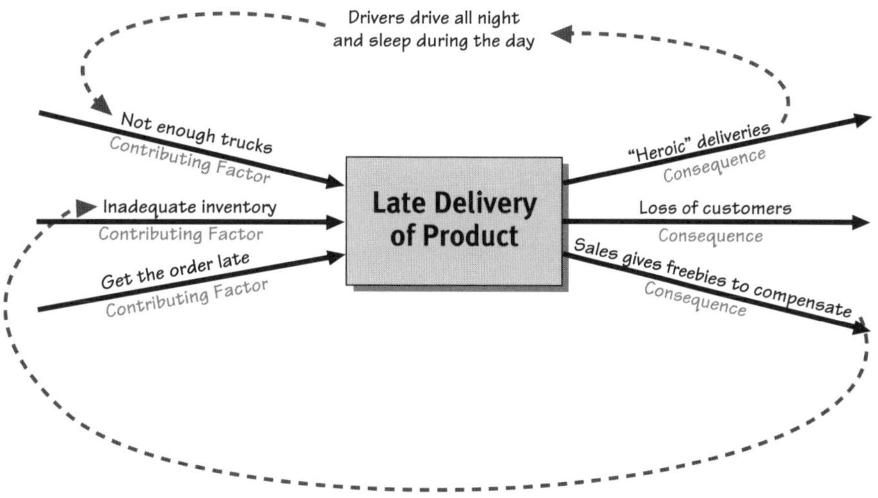

The second tool, called an "Inter-Action Map" (taught to me by Bob Putnam of Action Design), helps recovering knowers see their own contribution to seemingly intractable interpersonal stalemates. Participants in this activity start by filling in the box describing the other person's actions—what they were actually observed saying or doing. Then the participants fill in what they were thinking and feeling inside when they observed the other party's actions. Next, they fill in what actions they actually took in response to their own thoughts. And finally, they fill in the box for what the other person must have been thinking and feeling at the time. This box may take some consideration because it must, first of all, be a reasonable response to the participant's actions, and second, describe the thinking that would create the actions the other part produced. (See Figure 7-9 for an example of a completed Inter-Action Map.)

Figure 7-8

Inter-Action Map Template

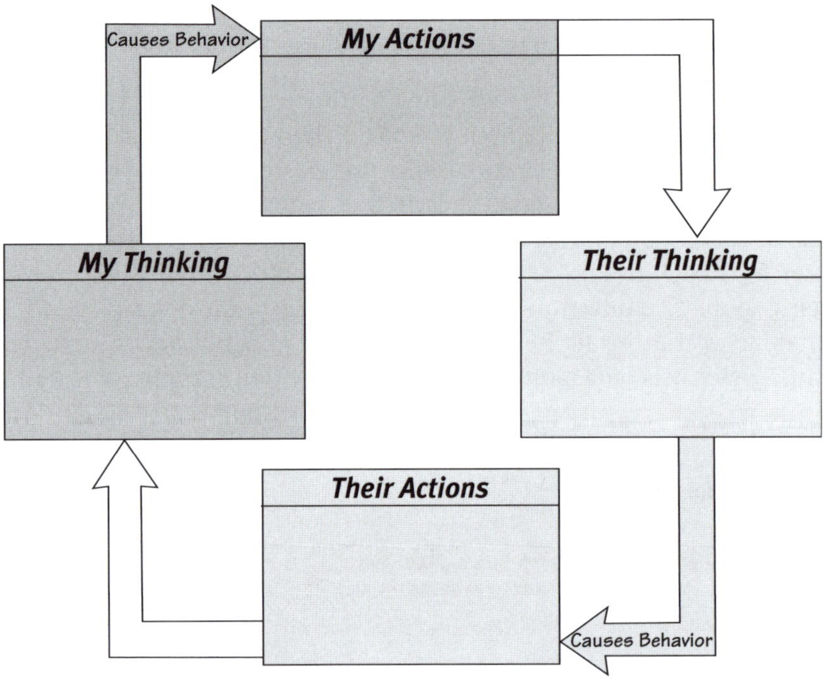

Figure 7-9

Inter-Action Map Example

```
                    ┌──────────────────────┐
                    │   Group's Actions    │
                    │                      │
              ┌────→│   Group members      │────┐
              │     │   don't participate. │    │
              │     └──────────────────────┘    │
              │                                 ▼
   ┌──────────────────────┐         ┌──────────────────────┐
   │   Group's Thinking   │         │    Chair's Thinking  │
   │                      │         │                      │
   │  "The chairperson    │         │   "These group       │
   │  doesn't want our    │         │   members            │
   │  input. Let's just   │         │   don't care."       │
   │  wait to be told     │         │                      │
   │  what to do."        │         │                      │
   └──────────────────────┘         └──────────────────────┘
              ▲                                 │
              │     ┌──────────────────────┐    │
              │     │   Chair's Actions    │    │
              │     │                      │    │
              └─────│  Chairperson makes   │←───┘
                    │  decisions and gives │
                    │  direction to        │
                    │  group members.      │
                    └──────────────────────┘
```

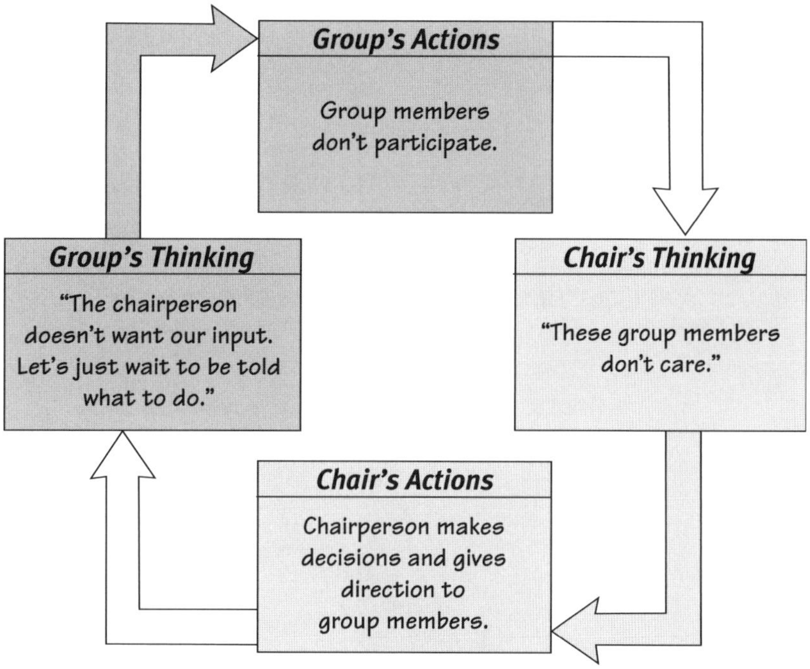

LOOK DEEPER

Concepts such as the "Iceberg model" (see Figure 7-10), a classic systems thinking tool, helped me understand that there are structures underlying the patterns that continue to cause the problems we keep seeing. If I look at the problem structures rather than at the problem event, I can develop more effective solutions Using the iceberg tool uncovers potential places for interventions, when previously, there didn't appear to be any.

When participants use the iceberg tool, they ask themselves a series of questions about the problem situation. First, they ask, "What happened?" This reveals the symptoms that show up above the waterline and are visible out there in the organization. Second, they ask, "What continues to happen?" to reveal the patterns involved, which also are visible. The third question they ask is, "What causes this pattern to be maintained?" Now they are getting at the structures of the problem, which are not usually tangible. The structures that hold patterns of behavior in place might be the formal organizational hierarchy, the culture of "niceness" that pervades the organization, the almost hypnotizing effect a certain manager has on her subordinates, and so on.

Just getting this far is often very effective, without going any deeper. At this point, hidden structures are revealed, perhaps for the first time. Now, the recovering knowers involved in this process must ask themselves, "Is *this* (structure) something I am willing to address?" Even though they were unwilling to address the problem before, this newly revealed structure has a known connection to the original problem. Through this route, a recovering knower may have discovered

Figure 7-10

Iceberg Diagram

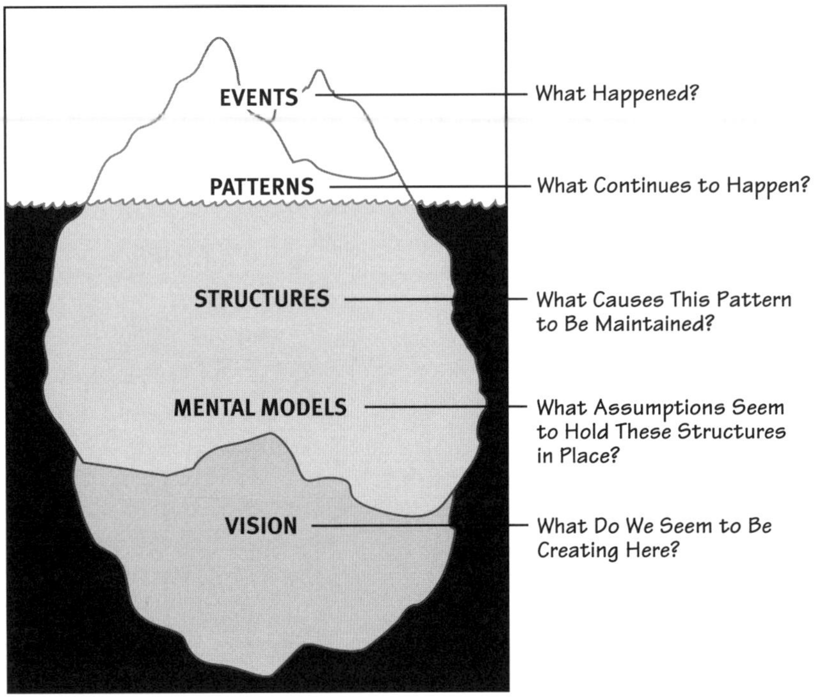
EVENTS
What Happened?
PATTERNS
What Continues to Happen?
STRUCTURES
What Causes This Pattern to Be Maintained?
MENTAL MODELS
What Assumptions Seem to Hold These Structures in Place?
VISION
What Do We Seem to Be Creating Here?

a different way to take the learner's stance and try a new action strategy. By the way, an intervention at this level is closely aligned with single-loop learning.

But why stop there? Why not move on to double- and triple-loop learning with the next two questions, respectively? When recovering knowers answer the next question, "What assumptions seem to hold these structures in place?" they will reveal the mental models that are at play in this situation. Examining and replacing mental models is a highly effective intervention. Then recovering knowers can go even deeper to the rarely used question, "What do we seem to be creating here?" Grappling with this question will tap into deep beliefs and visions held by individuals, groups, or the organization as a whole. Interventions at these last two levels are potentially ground-breaking and are deliberately achieved through deep reflection, followed by profound actions.

The power of systems thinking does not stop at looking deeper and looking wider. These systems thinking tools provided me with the biggest leverage point of all—the acknowledgment that I have contributed to a problem myself. For a knower, seeing myself as part of the problem is the most threatening aspect of any of the concepts from the five disciplines. And yet, systems thinking tools can help alleviate this effect, too. When I used tools such as causal loop and iceberg diagrams, I was able to objectify the problem by seeing the dynamics on paper, as a diagram, allowing me to take a more objective view. Now the problem becomes the thing on the paper that we are all looking at together—it's no longer *my* problem, it's *our* problem. Additionally, systems thinking helps me see my contribution to problems as part of a broader web of interconnections and influences rather than as just my individual mistake. With these tools, I demonstrate to myself and my colleagues that my contribution was not a neglectful or willful act but a reasonable response to conditions/influences I experienced at that time.

So, to overcome the secret of focusing exclusively on your own little piece of the world, apply systems thinking tools such as causal and Doom loops, Inter-Action maps, and the Iceberg model. As you do, your current "problems" will become interconnections and influences in a broad web of relationships. When you begin to see through a systems lens, you will naturally avoid blaming, turf wars, and self-imposed, imaginary boundaries.

From Protection to Reflection

Have you ever had conversations in which you sensed, at a certain point, that the other person was getting defensive, raising their voice, pressing their point, or proving that they were right and you were wrong? Or did you sense these kinds of reactions in yourself? Generally, those conversations do not end well. The point of Chapter 4's Activity 4 (page 41) was to give you a glimpse into your own tendency to protect rather than reflect during difficult conversations. You saw how it is quite natural, and unconscious, for us to fall into having conversations in protection mode. This can be traced back to the knower's secret thinking habit that says "protect myself during conversations."

MENTAL MODELS

Knowers feel they must protect what they know—they can't be wrong or have incomplete knowledge. Through the discipline of mental models, however, I have come to admit that there are multiple views on a given subject, and that these other views can be valid and rational, too. With this in mind, I can move from having conversations in protection mode to having them in reflection mode. In protection mode, I believe that I must protect the "fact" that I am right, that I have all the information I need, that I have not contributed to this problem. In reflection mode, I ponder my thinking and actions, and ask questions such as, "Why did I react so strongly just now?" "What information am I missing?" and "Have I somehow contributed to this problem?" Operating in reflection mode is a huge leap for knowers to make.

Concepts such as the "left-hand column" and "ladder of inference" (from Chris Argyris's *Overcoming Organizational Defenses*) helped me to discover a new way to understand how people think and interact—great information for a recovering knower! These techniques, mental frameworks, and exercises take some of the mystery out of difficult conversation; they allow me to talk productively with people, without feeling totally out of control. (See "The Way Conversations Work" section on page 80 for a detailed explanation.)

As a good knower armed with a new understanding of "the way conversations work," I set out to conquer the conversational world. I got a rude awakening. These conversational concepts only work in reflection mode—they give me a way to seek *mutual* understanding. They don't actually provide a way to win a conversational dispute. In fact, if you try to use these tools in a battle of words, you will be at a disadvantage—they make you weaker. So, while I was trying to have conversations in reflection mode, and the other person was using protection mode, it felt as though I was losing the battle. But then I gained another insight: If I am framing this conversation in terms of a battle, then it must mean that I am trying to win and that I am still operating in protection mode. Ouch! I had to continually remind myself that these conversational concepts only work in reflection mode.

By earnestly using these tools over time, I was able to move most of my disagreements from conflictual conversations to comparative conversations. At first, I was suspicious of practicing the discipline of mental models, because I thought it would somehow trick me into giving up, or losing, my view, thus creating my own identity quake. (An "identity quake" is a sudden shaking of your sense of self; the idea is described in *Difficult Conversations: How to Discuss What Matters Most*, by Douglas Stone, Bruce Patton, and Sheila Heen.) Instead, practicing the discipline of mental models helped me *loosen* my view. I began to realize that "I" am not "my view." I am a person who *has* a view. Armed with this understanding, it is not as threatening for a knower to embark on a conversation in which his view will be challenged. Because I am not my view, an attack on my view is not an attack on me. I can hold another view in one hand (metaphorically speaking) and my view in the other, and compare the two. I may even decide that I like pieces of the other view better, and if not, I'll just give them back. It is not as threatening to compare views as it is to battle for who's got "the right view." Using this process, I didn't have to protect my perspective so vigorously, and I could reflect on both ways of thinking and gain new insights.

So, to overcome the secret of having to protect yourself during conversations, apply these reflective conversational concepts. You will learn to increase reciprocal understanding, consider multiple viewpoints, and reduce your, and the other person's, defensiveness.

THE WAY CONVERSATIONS WORK

The ability to be aware of your own thinking (and then having productive conversations with that awareness) is foundational to all the other practices described in this book. Therefore, I'd like to give this issue a little more "airtime" and unpack it in more detail. The pieces of this discussion will be reconstructed here in a logical, step-by-step fashion, even though they came together for me only after years of scattered (and determined) study and practice.

Many participants in difficult conversations start with a predetermined conclusion or judgment about the other person or situation. For example, you may start a conversation with your teenage daughter with the mindset that she is lazy, or one with your coworker thinking that he is irresponsible. This approach is a recipe for making things worse. But the amazing thing is that you often don't even realize that you are having the conversation in order to prove that your conclusion about them is correct. You are likely to be unaware of this menacing predisposition.

Figure 7-11

Left-Hand Column Exercise

Left-Hand	Right-Hand
What we think and feel (but don't say)	What we say and do

A helpful way to uncover your undetected thoughts is to perform what Chris Argyris calls a "left-hand column exercise." (You can "play along" with this exercise as I describe it, if you wish.) First, draw a line down the middle of a sheet of paper. Recalling an irritating, troublesome, and important conversation you recently had with someone, on the right side of the line, jot down what each party actually said, as if you were transcribing a recording of your conversation. After that, on the left side of the page, next to the actual words that produced your reaction, write down what you were thinking and feeling at the time, but not saying. There, revealed in black and white, on the left side of the page, are your judgments and conclusions. This may be a surprise, but you actually have them! These hidden thoughts, or your inner voice, if you will, are known, simply, as your "left-hand column."

Now, look at your page again, and notice how what you were thinking and feeling at the time (left-hand column) had an impact on what you chose to, or chose not to, say or do (right-hand column). Most of the time, you can see a direct connection between your thoughts and actions. We can take it one step further, though, and suggest that your thoughts affected your actions, which affected the results of your conversation. You will recall that I asked you to start out this exercise with an "irritating, troublesome, and important conversation." That was a set-up. Because of this framing, we already know that the result of your conversation was negative. And, where did this negative result begin? With your thoughts!

So, the next question to answer, in this process of learning to have more productive conversations, is "How did those thoughts get there (in my left-hand column)?" Argyris uses a tool, called the "ladder of inference," to answer that question (see Figure 7-12). The ladder, metaphorically speaking, stands on a platform of directly observable data. All that the two parties said and did lies at the foot of the ladder. The human mind can't take in and comprehend all that goes on around us, so we have to be selective in what we pay attention to. In climbing the ladder of inference—making sense of what is happening around you—you have to start out by selecting what data to be conscious of. On this first rung, you will recall what you observed—what the other person actually said or did. (This requires the same skill you used to fill in the right-hand column, earlier.) Then,

Figure 7-12

Ladder of Inference

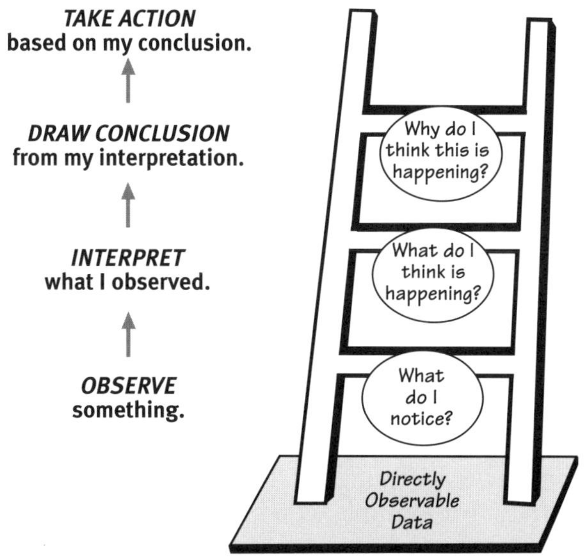

on the second rung, you reestablish how you interpreted what you observed—the meaning you added to your observations. And finally, on the third rung, you bring to mind the conclusion you drew about the person or situation, based on the interpretation you made about their behavior. So, where did those judgments and conclusions come from? You created them! You saw the other party behave in a certain way, and, using the ladder of inference, deemed their actions inappropriate, lazy, honorable, irrelevant, or whatever.

So, if you are the one who created your left-hand column, then it seems reasonable that you can also be the one to change it. You can remove the toxic thoughts that are ruining your conversations and replace them with healthy thoughts. How do you do it? I have two strategies to suggest: (1) Consider multiple stories—not just your own story, and (2) Move your conversations as low on the ladder as possible—that is, stick close to what you can observe.

Consider Multiple Stories

One of the most common errors knowers make in their conversations is what I call the *truth trap*. This error occurs when they assume they know "the truth, the whole truth, and nothing but the truth." Knowers will go on to explain: "Oh yeah, and I know all I need to know. There is only one correct story, and of course, that one is mine. One more thing: I am certain about this."

Who *does* have the right story, and how do you decide? This is the wrong question to ask. An incredible amount of time and energy is wasted debating whose story has more merit. You can avoid the truth trap with two powerful tools: the "AND stance," and the "3rd story" (both of these tools are described in *Difficult Conversations: How to Discuss What Matters Most*).

The AND stance is a tool for avoiding all-or-nothing thinking where it is assumed there is only one "correct" view. You may have heard the phrase, "'But' is the great erasure." What this means is when you are discussing two different points of view and you link them with the word "but," everything spoken before the "but" will be erased from the listener's consciousness. For example, if I am your boss and I say to you, "I love the detailed analysis you put into that report, as well as how you presented it at the meeting, but because you arrived late, you lost credibility." You are probably now thinking that you blew it, and you are a bad employee, because you lost credibility. Do you even remember that I praised you for the report and the presentation?

Go back and read that quote again, this time, substituting the word "but" with "and." It has a different feel to it, doesn't it? Now, you see yourself as a more complex worker: You are the kind of worker who gives good presentations, creates detailed reports, and sometimes arrives late to meetings. The presentations and reports increase your credibility and arriving late reduces your credibility. Recovering knowers should embrace the idea of multiple views and move from the stance of one truth to multiple perceptions.

The 3rd story is a tool that describes a different views in a disagreement in such a way that both parties can simultaneously agree with it. The 3rd story is the story a neutral observer might tell. It captures the difference between the two stories and yet binds them together in a way that can be a great starting point to reconcile them. The magic phrase that will encapsulate the 3rd story starts with: "We seem to have different views about . . . ." Then you complete the phrase by naming the two perspectives. For example, you might say, "We seem to have different views about what constitutes a 'long wait' for our customers. I think that

15 minutes is too long, and you think 30 minutes is reasonable. I wonder if we could talk about what is behind these perspectives?" Another example: "We seem to have different views about what type of pet to have in our house. You would like a dog because you had one growing up and they are warm, loyal companions. I would like a cat because they basically take care of themselves, and they don't create a mess. Can we talk more about what qualities would be a nice fit for our family?"

Move Your Conversations As Low on the Ladder As Possible

Another common error we make in our conversations is what I call *ladder leaping*. Knowers leap up to the top of the ladder of inference and conduct most of their conversations at the level of conclusions, rarely coming back down to confirm the data or test their interpretations. They treat their assumptions and conclusions as if they are "facts." Here is an example of how their thinking goes: "I saw Brenda spit her gum out. And people who spit their gum out are uncouth. Therefore, Brenda is uncouth."

Imagine that two colleagues, Carl and Dee, are walking toward each other in the hallway. Carl sees Dee coming and is expecting to greet her as they usually do. This is especially important to him this morning, in light of that meeting last night, where Dee seemed quite miffed with him after he disagreed with her. When Dee comes within 30 feet of Carl, she suddenly lowers her head, turns her face toward the wall, slows down, and passes Carl without saying hello. Carl had just inhaled to say "good morning," when he saw Dee turn her head, so he walked on by, thinking, "She is so rude." Later, they talked about this exchange:

Take 1

Carl: Hi Dee. I'd like to talk to you about something. Do you have a minute?

Dee: Sure Carl. What's up?

Carl: Well . . . I'll just come right out with it . . . I'd like to talk to you about why you've been so rude to me lately.

Dee: What do you mean? I don't know what are you're talking about!

Carl: Oh, really? You seem to have a chip on your shoulder the last few days. All of a sudden you don't want to talk to me anymore?

Dee: What do mean? We talked last night at the meeting.

Carl: Yeah—if you call that "talking." What about dissing me this morning?

Dee: What? I didn't even talk to you this morning! Are you just making stuff up so you can zing me again, like last night?!

Carl: See? This is exactly what I'm talking about! You are so rude! I'm outta here!

This conversation started out bad and got worse because Carl started his conversation at the top of the ladder—with his conclusions. Figure 7-13 shows the contents of Carl's ladder of inference. He observed that Dee looked down and remained quiet. He interpreted that to mean she wanted to ignore him. His interpretation also included a perspective that people shouldn't ignore others when passing them in the hallway, so what she did wasn't right. And based on that interpretation, he concluded that Dee is rude because she ignored him. Because Carl started the conversation with his conclusions, Dee felt like she was being

Figure 7-13

Carl's Ladder of Inference

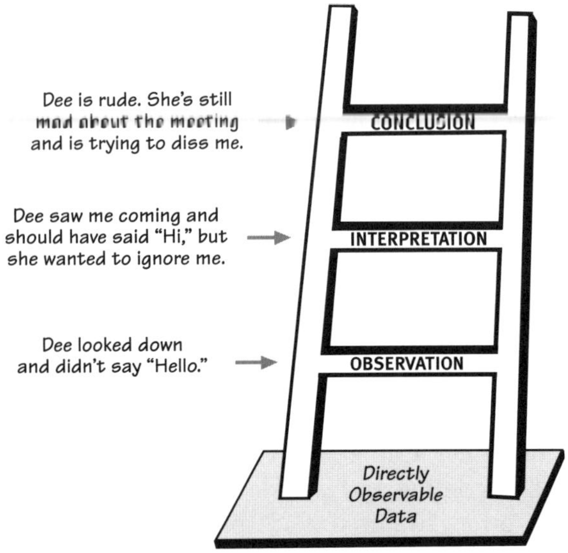
Dee is rude. She's still mad about the meeting and is trying to diss me.
CONCLUSION
Dee saw me coming and should have said "Hi," but she wanted to ignore me.
INTERPRETATION
Dee looked down and didn't say "Hello."
OBSERVATION
Directly Observable Data

attacked, became defensive, and fought back. Having conversations at the top of the ladder is one of the worst things you can do if you want them to lead to mutual understanding and a better relationship. Let's try this conversation again—this time from the bottom of the ladder—and see what happens.

Take 2

Carl: Hi Dee. I'd like to talk to you about something. Do you have a minute?

Dee: Sure Carl. What's up?

Carl: Well . . . Earlier today, when we were about to pass each other in the hallway, you suddenly looked down and away from me, and didn't say anything to me. Do you remember that?

Dee: I think so . . . Oh yeah. That was in the hallway with the big windows, right?

Carl: Right. Maybe this is no big deal, but I wanted to test it with you anyway. Usually, you say "Hi" to me, and considering that we disagreed pretty aggressively last night, I was thinking to myself that you might be angry with me and wanted to ignore me this morning. Is that what was going on?

Dee: Oh, no—no. I remember now. I saw you coming toward me, and I was prepared to say "Hi," but then something glistening on the floor caught my eye. I had lost my diamond earring last week, and I couldn't believe that there it was in the corner, next to the wall! So I wasn't ignoring you, I was just retrieving my earring.

Carl: Oh! I see. That's good. I'm glad I talked to you about this, otherwise I'd still be thinking you were trying to diss me. [laughs] Our relationship is important to me, and after last night's meeting, I am particularly sensitive to how we're getting along.

Dee: Oh, don't worry about it. You'd have to do a lot worse things in a meeting in order to get on my bad list. [laughs]

Carl starts at the bottom of the ladder this time. He shares what he noticed—the directly observable data—and then confirms that Dee observed the same things. So far, so good. They already have their first agreement. Then he has to take a little bit of a risk by sharing his interpretation of what he observed—he could be wrong. When he shares the meaning he gave to her actions, he invites her to share her interpretation, too. She does, and now they can compare views. Notice one significant thing about this second take—no one mentions the word "rude." If that was Carl's conclusion, why didn't he say it?

It amazes me with all the difficult conversations I have participated in, coached others for, or facilitated as a neutral party, rarely is it necessary to reach the conclusion level to increase mutual understanding. So many conversations and relationships could be improved if the parties would just stick to their data, and their interpretation of that data, and then just compare views. Not much more is needed. When recovering knowers stay low on the ladder of inference, feelings are diffused, and there is much less defensiveness. It is pretty hard to get upset or defensive over data. The conclusions and judgments are what hurt feelings and create defensiveness.

Figure 7-14 depicts the structure of conversations. Notice how this closed loop works. You start at the bottom of the ladder where something happens. Then you

Figure 7-14

The Structure of Conversations

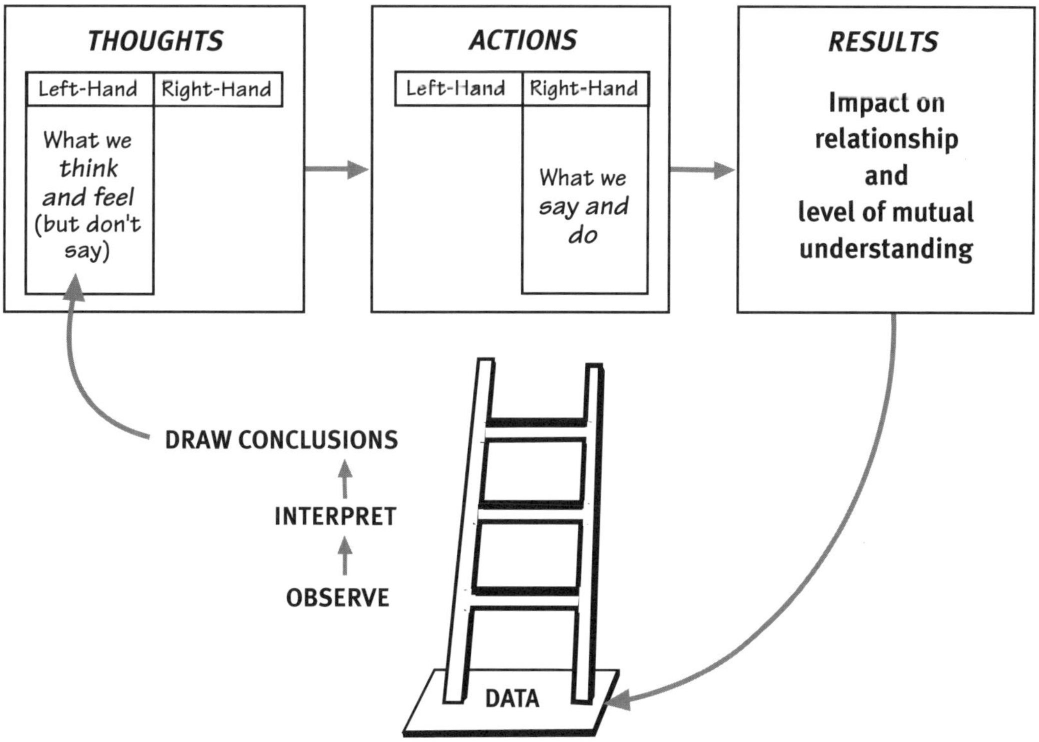

interpret and draw a conclusion about what you noticed. You tuck that conclusion you just created into your left-hand column, where it impacts the actions you take and, ultimately, the results you get. The results of the conversation become the data for the next round of interpretation, conclusion, action, and results.

I can summarize what you can glean from this diagram with three statements. (1) Your thinking (left-hand column) has an impact on the results of your conversations. (2) You create your own left-hand column (with the ladder of inference), and therefore possess great leverage to improve your conversations. (3) Your left-hand column can be changed by effectively using the ladder of inference.

From Debate to Mutual Learning

Some work teams successfully complete their projects in a minimum amount of time, with few resources, and with little interpersonal hassle. The goal was completely clear and attainable, all the necessary information was readily available, and the time demands were manageable. Have you ever been a part of such a team? There is something satisfying about being a member of a group that accomplishes its task smoothly and efficiently. Often, something is missing from such a team, though. Call it mystery; call it exploration; call it discovery. This group was operating completely in the realm of the knowable, measurable, and describable. But because the world is constantly changing, over time, what once was knowable, measurable, and describable becomes obsolete. Without creating new insights and discoveries, you will see the problems you formerly "solved" resurface, sometimes with a vengeance.

In Activity 5 of Chapter 4 (page 45), you may have experienced a little of the difference between conversations focused on deciding and those focused on exploring or discovering new insights. This activity gave you several chances to choose debate mode or mutual-learning mode—choices we face on a day-to-day basis. I am sad to say that, as a knower, I often prefer debate mode or trying to help others "decide already!" The secret thinking habit that puts me in this position is the belief that I must debate and direct during group interactions.

TEAM LEARNING

The essence of team learning is developing our ability to move from debating who has "the truth" to generating collective insights together. When I debate, I am pursuing the "right" answer—the truth that lies within the realm of the things I know. We run into trouble, however, when what is known becomes outdated as the world rapidly changes around us. At times like these, when we play the same roles and spout the same truisms, debating who has the right knowledge simply doesn't move the group forward. Therefore, it is necessary to generate new insights in order to make progress—and to do so in a way that does not threaten myself or other members of the team.

To stimulate team learning, turn to the conversational technique called "dialogue," which is particularly valuable for generating collective insight. (Many fine books about the practice of dialogue are available, including *Dialogue: The Art of Thinking Together*, by William Isaacs, and *The Magic of Dialogue*, by Daniel

Yankelovich.) As I began to try out ways to generate collective insight, I realized that at a certain critical point in our progress, there was, literally, nothing to debate. Because we were seeking "emerging knowledge," ideas that have not yet fully emerged, it was literally impossible to debate the "right" emerging knowledge. It all just emerges. When new ideas are being revealed, there is no debate. We just say to ourselves, "Oh, there's a new one. And, look, here comes another idea." When the group reverted back to debating, it was because new thoughts and reflections had ceased to emerge, and we were left with our old biases, assumptions, and perspectives. We know that a team has a high aptitude for team learning when debate is being replaced with suspension of judgment, and when meaningful discussion flows freely among the members of the group.

Team learning can be threatening to knowers, because they thrive in debate mode. They direct the conversations to the topics *they* want to talk about and proceed to confound others with their skilled point/counterpoint debates, or else they mentally "check out." Asking knowers to give up debate and become immersed in a process of mutual inquiry makes them feel uncomfortable and out of control.

Team learning does have some attractive and practical qualities for knowers, however. Knowers are always interested in discovering new knowledge; they just have to overcome a hesitancy to accept knowledge coming from someone else. Dialogue can also be used as part of a problem-solving process, but it should not be employed for making any final decisions—if used, it must precede decision-making. In addition, team learning is a great way to introduce collective responsibility to a group ("How did we each contribute?"), which is particularly attractive to knowers, who are sensitive to being blamed.

Figure 7-15

From Knower to Learner with the Five Disciplines

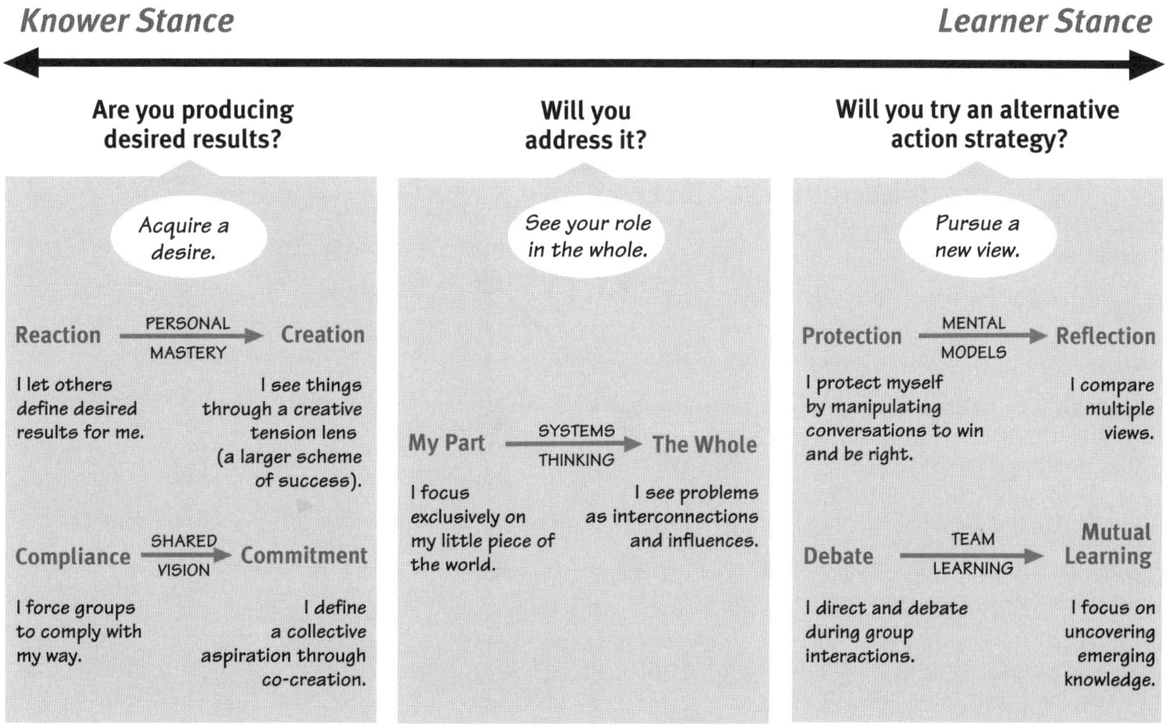
Knower Stance
Learner Stance
Are you producing desired results?
Will you address it?
Will you try an alternative action strategy?
Acquire a desire.
See your role in the whole.
Pursue a new view.
Reaction
PERSONAL MASTERY
Creation
I let others define desired results for me.
I see things through a creative tension lens (a larger scheme of success).
Compliance
SHARED VISION
Commitment
I force groups to comply with my way.
I define a collective aspiration through co-creation.
My Part
SYSTEMS THINKING
The Whole
I focus exclusively on my little piece of the world.
I see problems as interconnections and influences.
Protection
MENTAL MODELS
Reflection
I protect myself by manipulating conversations to win and be right.
I compare multiple views.
Debate
TEAM LEARNING
Mutual Learning
I direct and debate during group interactions.
I focus on uncovering emerging knowledge.

So, to overcome the secret habit of directing and debating during group interactions, apply the group conversational techniques of team learning. You will develop the skill to move these conversations from debate to mutual learning, and generate meaningful new insights, even when the issue is not easily knowable, measurable, or describable.

Figure 7-15, "From Knower to Learner with the Five Disciplines," illustrates how these disciplines assist you in successfully answering the first three Learner's Path questions and nicely summarizes this process. Practicing personal mastery and shared vision can help you *acquire a desire,* and therefore help you successfully answer Question 1. Practicing systems thinking can help you *see your role in the whole,* and thereby successfully answer Question 2. And practicing mental models and team learning can help you *pursue a new view,* and thereby successfully answer Question 3.

Will You Be Ready?

As Alvin Toffler wrote in the forward to *Rethinking the Future,* by Rowen Gibson, "The illiterate of the 21st century will not be those who cannot read and write, but those who cannot learn, unlearn, and relearn." Can you imagine that day when people's competence is based not on their ability to be knowers but on their ability to learn, unlearn, and relearn? Will you be ready? Will you be "literate"? By understanding the pitfalls of remaining a knower and diligently practicing the five disciplines, you will place yourself squarely on the path to success in the twenty-first century.

Figure 7-4

Solution to the Nine Dots Puzzle

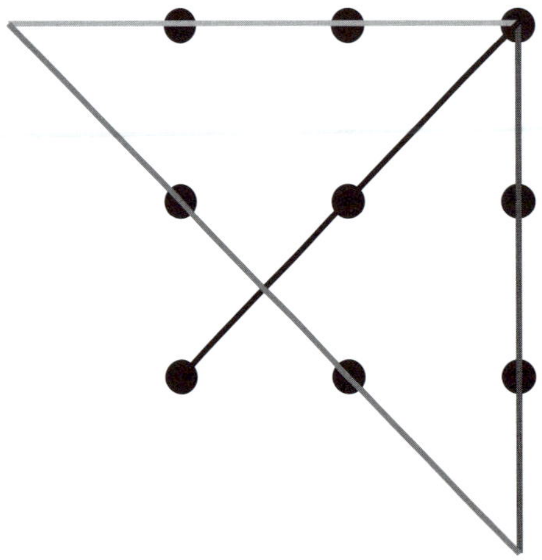

Rapid Recap

- To change the thinking habits of a knower into thinking habits of a learner (or to overcome the secrets of a knower), it is necessary to make progress along five learning continuums:
    - From a reactive orientation to a creative orientation *(personal mastery)*
    - From a compliance mentality to a commitment mentality *(shared vision)*
    - From "my part" thinking to "the whole" thinking *(systems thinking)*
    - From protection-mode conversations to reflection-mode conversations *(mental models)*
    - From debate to mutual learning *(team learning)*
- The five learning disciplines have a dual purpose: for a knower to *become* a learner and for a learner to develop further *as* a learner.

Reflective Response

- Which of the five disciplines seems to resonate with you the most?
    - Why?
- Which of the five continuums presents the greatest challenge to your progress?

Chapter 8
Pulling It All Together

When you read a self-help or advice book on how to improve your life and your organization, do you ever think, "That is so cool. I need to apply that advice to my life"? But then, once you put the book down, are you disappointed when nothing much in your life changes? Why doesn't your life change? Because the advice is not given in a way that is actionable—that shows you how to implement it. Chapters 1 through 7 of this book show you how to identify your knower and learner tendencies, understand the structure and process of learning, uncover secret thinking habits, and transform from a knower into a learner; this chapter shows you how to make it all *happen*.

Recovering knowers will not give up their old ways just because they think organizational learning is a good idea. *I* thought the disciplines of organizational learning were great when I was introduced to them, but I got stuck and didn't understand why when I tried to implement some of the practices. When I taught the five learning disciplines, my students would have a great experience with the material, gaining both an intellectual understanding and a heartfelt desire to use the practices; but then, weeks later, they hadn't implemented any of the concepts. I didn't understand this, either. So, I went on a quest to understand and discovered the Learner's Path.

Actionable Advice

The framework presented here makes the practice of the five disciplines actionable in two ways: (1) It is based on the touchstone of achievement of desired results; and (2) The Learner's Path questions force us to increase our awareness of what we are doing and then make a choice in response to that information.

TOUCHSTONE

The common definition of "learning," which I have discussed (and rejected) previously, is "increasing the amount of information in one's head." Using this definition, it is relatively easy to say "I have learned the five disciplines." For example, you might be able to call yourself a systems thinker if you intellectually understand the tools and concepts, and can even explain them to others. It is another thing altogether to say that you are a systems thinker when the definition of learning is "increasing one's ability to achieve desired results." In this second case, you would have to make public your evidence for being a systems thinker by demonstrating how the use of the systems thinking tools and concepts actually helped you to achieve a desired result. This is the true touchstone, or test, for having learned something. You can't keep the learning hidden away in your head. Learning is not private property.

AWARENESS AND CHOICE

Fred Kofman has a compelling way of thinking about awareness and choice (terms that are discussed in *Conscious Business*). Learning, for him, is closing the gap between what you are creating and what you would like to create. He describes the process of learning as an expansion of consciousness and of your capacity to be aware and to make choices using that awareness. The very act of paying attention and responding to the Learner's Path questions increases our awareness. Then we must choose our answer. In order to become a learner, we must answer these questions successfully, and we must be willing to say so in front of others. Nothing is more actionable than making a choice.

A Map for Moving Forward

Now that the progression from knower to learner has been thoroughly explained, it is time to make a choice. What are you going to do with this information? As you read at the beginning of this chapter, you can't claim to have learned anything until you have taken action and seen its effect on your desired results. To guide you on your next move, review the chart on page 93, which summarizes the transformational process described in this book. Consider it your map to navigate from knower to learner.

To use the chart, (1) select a challenging area in your life that continually presents itself to you; or (2) ask a friend, colleague, or family member to suggest an area where they think you could make some improvement. The second way is more risky yet much more powerful. Then just progress from left to right across the columns, guided by the words below:

- **Learner's Path Questions.** The left-most column starts with the first three awareness-raising questions from the Learner's Path. Knowers will get stuck answering one of these questions (typically, if it means sharing their true answer with others). Learners will breeze through these questions (and possibly move on to Questions 4 and 5).
- **Typical (Unsuccessful) Answers.** Here, recovering knowers can locate their particular answer to each of the Learner's Path questions and identify which question causes them to get stuck.
- **Knower's Secret Thinking Habits.** Use this column to diagnose which secret thinking habit has led to the unsuccessful answers noted in the second column. This is where individual and group issues are identified as well.

- **Willingness Needed to Overcome Secret Thinking Habits.** This is another moment of choice for recovering knowers, who must decide whether or not they are willing to make the commitment described in this column.
- **Primary Learning Discipline.** If knowers are willing to commit to overcoming their secret thinking habit, then this column identifies the learning discipline they will need to practice.
- **Abilities of a Recovering Knower.** This column describes the ability, or capacity, that a recovering knower must develop to overcome the secret thinking habit. This is the gateway through which one moves from being a knower to becoming a learner.
- **Essential Tools.** The recovering knower uses these tools to develop the ability to become a learner. There are many others to choose from, but these are the ones most in alignment with the five disciplines.

Learner's Path Question	Typical (Unsuccessful) Answers	Knower's Secret Thinking Habit	Willingness Needed to Overcome Secret Thinking Habit	Primary Learning Discipline	Abilities of a Recovering Knower	Essential Tools
1. Are you producing desired results?	• I don't know *what* I want. • I don't really care if I am producing desired results or not. • My results are fine—compared to other people's results. • To be honest, I'm just pretending that I *am* achieving desired results. • All I know are the results I *don't* want to see—what I want to get rid of.	Other people and circumstances define what my desired results ought to be.	Acquire a desire	Personal Mastery	Pulled by internal desire rather than pushed by external pressure.	• Creative orientation • Drawing forth personal vision and values
					• Use a structure for living from the creative orientation. • Contextualize success/failure.	Creative tension
		I force group members to comply with my way in order to get things done.	Acquire a desire (collectively)	Shared Vision	Generate commitment by co-creating collective aspiration.	Four essentials of shared vision
2. Will you address it?	• I don't have enough authority to address it. • It's not part of my job, therefore it's not my problem. • It's too big of a responsibility for me to handle. • I didn't make the mess, so I shouldn't have to clean it up.	I focus exclusively on my small piece of the world.	See your role in the whole	Systems Thinking	Look deeper and wider to see the web of interconnections and influences.	• Causal loops • Event/ Pattern/ Structure Iceberg
3. Will you try an alternative action strategy?	• I just don't know what to do next. • The pain of changing is greater than the pain of staying the same.	I protect myself during conversations.	Pursue a new view	Mental Models	Seek reciprocal understanding by considering multiple perspectives.	• Ladder of inference • Left-hand column
		I direct and debate during group interactions.	Pursue a new view (collectively)	Team Learning	Generate new collective insights through mutual learning.	Dialogue

Let's look at some sample responses:

- **You are getting stuck on Question 1.** You know this because you recognize your typical answer from the second column as "I don't really know what I want." You always do what other people want—you have no aspirations of your own. You see from the fourth column that you need to acquire a desire and focus on personal mastery, as the fifth column suggests. You want to develop the ability to be pulled by internal desire (sixth column), so you start working to develop a personal mission statement, which draws forth your vision and values (seventh column) and gives you renewed desire to accomplish what you want to accomplish.
- **You are stumped by Question 2.** You don't feel as though you have enough authority to address this situation, and you recognize this assumption as playing right into the secret thinking habit of focusing exclusively on your small piece of the world (third column). You conjure up your courage and decide to look deeper into your possible contribution to the problem (fourth column), which the map suggests should be addressed with systems thinking (fifth column). Again, you shift to the right from there to "Essential Tools," where the map suggests using the event/pattern/structure iceberg and causal loops (seventh column). You do so and discover your contribution is that you don't communicate effectively with your boss (who has the authority), so you resolve to address the situation by improving your communication.
- **You get stuck on Question 3.** The second column confirms that you are not taking new actions because the pain of changing is greater than the pain of staying the same. You recognize that you are protecting yourself during difficult conversations with a coworker (third column), and you need to pursue a new view through the practice of mental models (fifth column). The sixth column of the map suggests that you consider multiple perspectives, so you learn to use the ladder of inference and left-hand column tools. You become skillful at having difficult conversations, and your conversations improve with your coworker.

These are just a few examples of how you would go about using this map to improve the likelihood that you will successfully answer the first three questions of the Learner's Path.

Rapid Recap

- A self-guided map, covering the material from knower to learner, helps to make the wisdom and advice of this book actionable.

Reflective Response

- If you were to initially focus on one area on the map in your journey from knower to learner, what area would you choose? Why?

Chapter 9

Using the Learner's Path *As* a Learner

Up to now, this book has concentrated on teaching you how to overcome your knower tendencies to *become* a learner. This emphasis on *becoming* is meant to help the great majority of us who, from time to time, on certain issues, get stuck in the knower stance. This material can also be helpful, however, for an experienced, practicing learner. The Learner's Path, and the associated disciplines, frameworks, tools, and methods, have an even broader application than merely overcoming the secrets of a knower—they can be used *as* a learner to move you into double- and triple-loop learning, too. This chapter provides a description (albeit brief) of how advanced learners can utilize the Learner's Path to continue the momentum and depth of learning beyond the single-loop variety.

Dual Use of the Five Disciplines

The diagram on the next page (Figure 9-1) illustrates how the learning disciplines can serve two purposes. The disciplines are again listed under Questions 1 to 3 to show that they are used there to help readers answer the questions successfully and move from knower to learner (to *become* a learner). The arrows shown here, encompassing the disciplines and pointing to Questions 4 and 5, illustrate that the learning disciplines can be applied to answering an established learner's deeper questions as well.

To successfully answer Question 4, you will need to test the validity of your "winning strategy," a term borrowed from Robert Hargrove's *Masterful Coaching*. A "winning strategy" is a single-loop action strategy that you rely on and use frequently to achieve your *usual* results. The point of the fourth question, however, is to prepare you to achieve *unusual* results—higher-leverage, more effective outcomes. The five disciplines can help here as well. There is no particular discipline to help with this fourth question, because the one you choose will depend on the issue being addressed. For example, let's say that the winning strategy I usually employ whenever my team gets together is holding vigorous debates. If we only debate what we know rather than create breakthrough insights, then we would need to apply the discipline of team learning. Or, if my winning strategy for running an effective department is to focus exclusively on our internal operations rather than seeing the role of my

Figure 9-1

Dual Purpose of the Learning Disciplines

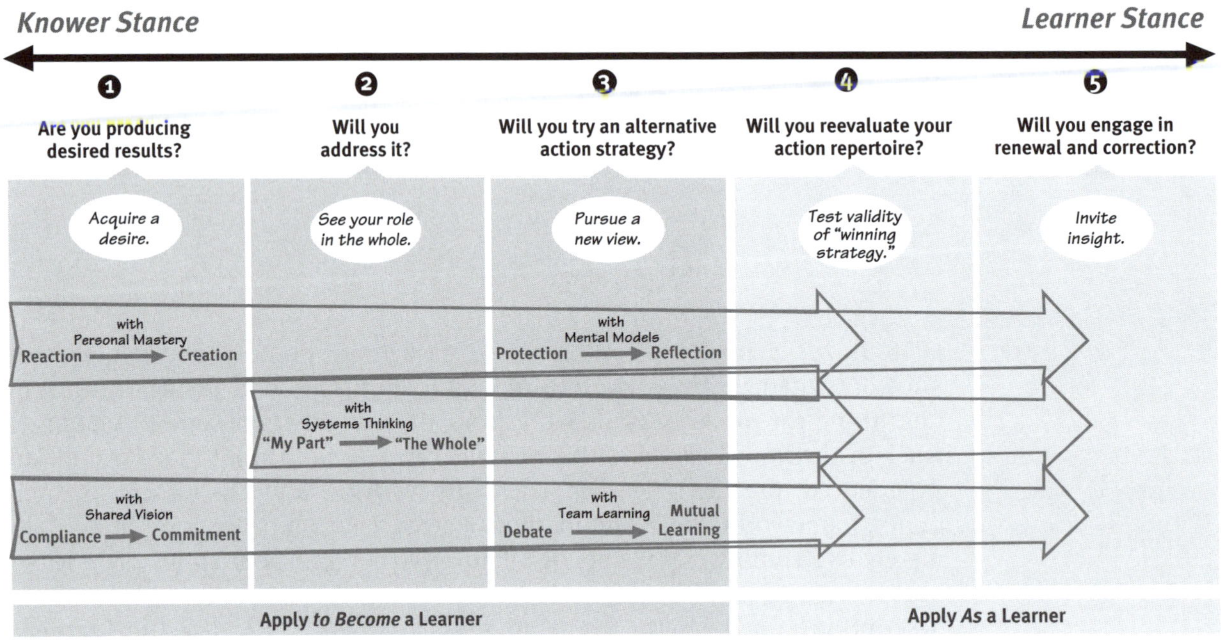

department in the whole, then I would need to apply the discipline of systems thinking. So, any or all of the disciplines could be applied at this stage to help you successfully answer Question 4 and move into double-loop learning.

To tackle Question 5, you will need to develop the ability to "invite insight." To invite insight means to open yourself up at a deep level for honest, and sometimes difficult, introspection regarding how "who you are" may be contributing to your not achieving your desired results. As in Question 4, deciding which discipline to apply at this juncture depends on the issue at hand. But, of all the questions to answer, this fifth question draws on principles and practices that include, but also go well beyond, the five disciplines. Inviting insight is deep and personal work; sometimes a single new insight can permanently change the trajectory of your life, your team, or your organization. This is precisely the nature of triple-loop learning.

Let me illustrate. For several months in 2005, Gerber Memorial Health Services was showing a financial loss. Various groups had attempted multiple improvement strategies, some single-loop and some double-loop in nature, but none seemed to stem the tide. I was developing the Learner's Path concept at that time and suggested to the top administrators that we convene a group to do some triple-loop reflection on this financial issue. They agreed. So they gathered a group of about 10 leaders, called the Triple-Loop Council, to invite insight into how we, as leaders, might be contributing to this financial crisis ourselves. This required deep introspection and brutal honesty with ourselves and with each other. As a result, we expressed a level of vulnerability and authenticity rarely seen in our organization. Together, we were committing to engage in renewal and correction.

Some of the characteristics that we noticed we had as leaders of this organization include the following: (1) We didn't like to utilize outside help; (2) We weren't empowering our front-line staff; and (3) We weren't acting like authentic leaders. After many months of closely working together and, as a group, exploring our contribution to the problem, we implemented a turnaround strategy based on these three triple-loop insights that has had a huge effect on our organization.

A Map for Transformation

The chart below summarizes the advanced steps (Questions 4 and 5) in the transformational process described in this chapter. As with the similar chart in Chapter 8 (page 93), begin at the left column and move across the page to the right. Start by asking yourself one of the advanced Learner's Path Questions. If you recognize that you are getting stuck at that question, progress across the page until you come to the column of "Essential Tools" that are recommended for overcoming the "Unproductive Thinking Habit" that keeps you stuck.

Notice that all five disciplines are listed as "Essential Tools" for Question 4. Practicing the five disciplines and learning in a double-loop format work hand-in-glove together. This is the realm in which I predominantly practiced the five

Learner's Path Question	Typical (Unsuccessful) Answers	Unproductive Thinking Habits	Willingness Needed to Overcome Thinking Habit	Primary Learning Concept	Abilities of a Learner	Essential Tools
4. Will you reevaluate your action repertoire?	• I just have to figure out (or have someone tell me) what to do differently. • I still have a few tricks up my sleeve. • I just need a little more know-how.	• I'm interested in know-how—not know-why (action—not reflection). • I'm afraid to reach the end of what I know how to do.	Test validity of winning strategies	Double-Loop Learning	Expand action repertoire through questioning and replacing obsolete assumptions about desired results and/or winning strategies.	• Personal Mastery practices • Shared Vision practices • Systems Thinking practices • Mental Models practices • Team Learning practices
5. Will you engage in renewal and correction?	• This is just who I am. • I don't think I want to go there.	• I am afraid to reach the end of myself. • I am my winning strategies • I'm all right—the world's all wrong.	Invite Insight	Triple-Loop Learning	• Expand action repertoire through deep self-assessment, and replacement of obsolete under-standings of your self-concept and action repertoire. • Feel secure in exploring what comes after reaching "the end of myself."	• Personal Mastery practices • Spiritual Development practices • Team Learning practices

disciplines for many years. And I continue to believe that one of the most powerful uses of the five disciplines is to promote and enable double-loop learning.

Deep Learning

Think of this chart as a map for navigating from a *learner* to a *deep learner,* or as a map for transformation. The difference between learners and deep learners is that learners draw from their existing action repertoire to try alternative action strategies (a good thing); deep learners expand their action repertoire and then try alternative action strategies (a better thing). Refer to the diagram "Moving On to Deeper Learning" to see how you can use the five disciplines for becoming a learner *and* for moving on to deeper learning.

Double- and triple-loop learning usually begin when a person has become a learner and sees the necessity and appeal of becoming a deep learner. A person who regularly engages in double-loop learning progresses from "trying again" (as single-loop learners do) to practicing "reflection-in-action." This is an ability to view the work you are doing from a "meta," or a more encompassing, transcendent perspective, as if you are floating above, watching yourself, considering the

Figure 9-2

Moving On to Deeper Learning

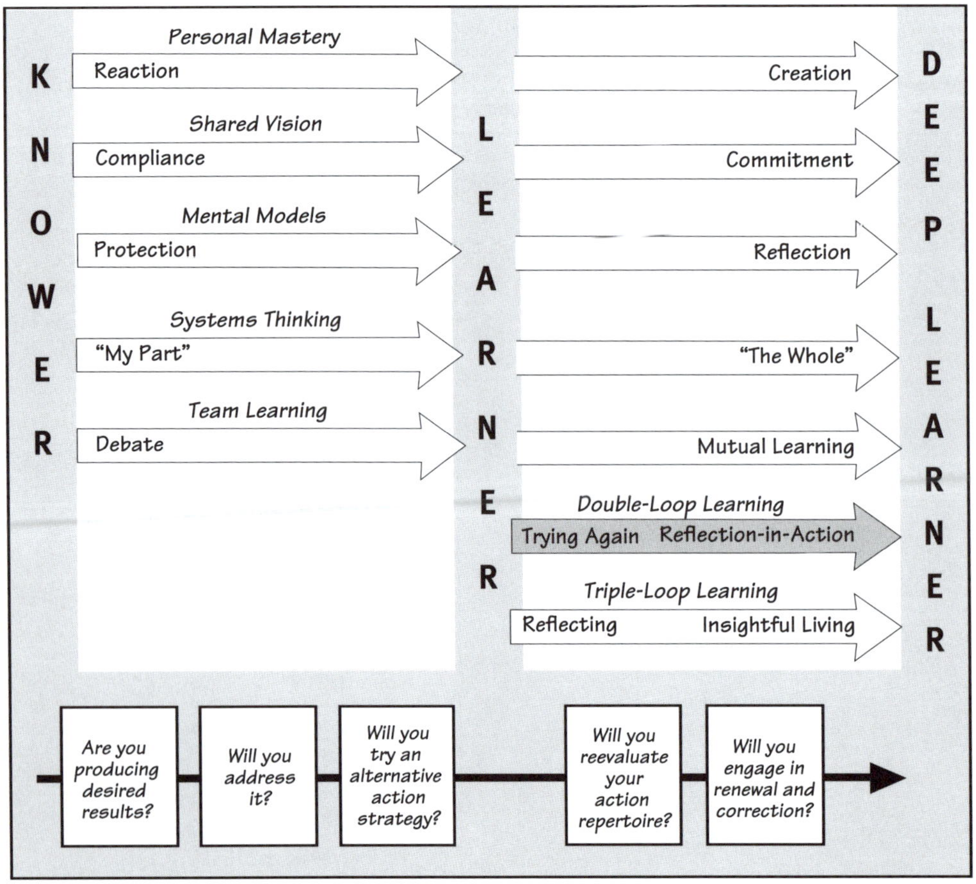

assumptions you are operating under. A person who regularly engages in triple-loop learning will progress from "reflecting" on his or her actions (as double-loop learners do) to "insightful living"—which is being in a constant state of renewal and correction.

People we might call authentic learners integrate the Learner's Path into their ongoing practice in a more advanced way. They see the early stages of the Learner's Path (Questions 1 to 3), not so much as an intensive exercise in overcoming their knower tendencies, but as a routine and natural part of a learning cycle, whether it is single-, double-, or triple-loop. These authentic learners quickly assimilate the Learner's Path questions into their habitual way of being in the world. They are not threatened by these questions but use them as routine reminders of how to continue with their learning rhythms. Authentic learners are not surprised when they come face to face with one of their knower tendencies—they even joke about it with other learners. This type of authentic learner is born out of a symbiotic relationship with a learning culture in which they can safely "not know."

The Learner's Path Decision Tree

The Learner's Path Decision Tree (Figure 9-3) integrates the material in this book; it is the positive antidote to the cynical "Knower Decision Tree" diagram (see Chapter 3, page 24). Notice that the five questions of the Learner's Path (see Chapter 5, page 49) are contained in the main diamonds and that everything cycles back through the home plate of learning (see Chapter 1, page 7). The "willingnesses" (see Chapter 8, page 93) necessary to successfully answer the questions are contained in the cloud icons. You will also see that, based on the decisions you make along the way, you will be navigating through single-, double-, or triple-loop learning (see Chapter 2, page 14 and following).

Figure 9-4 is a simplified version of the decision tree (Figure 9-3). Use either one of these diagrams as a constant reference companion. Pin a copy of it to the bulletin board next to your desk, as some of my friends and colleagues have done. Memorize it so that the Learner's Path Decision Tree is in your mind. Almost everything I do that requires me to respond to a change in the environment is filtered through this decision tree. When I'm faced with a challenge, I start an inner dialogue with myself, using this decision tree as a guide. Start viewing your change or learning opportunities through the Learner's Path framework, and see if you can dramatically increase your ability to achieve desired results.

Figure 9-3

Learner's Path Decision Tree

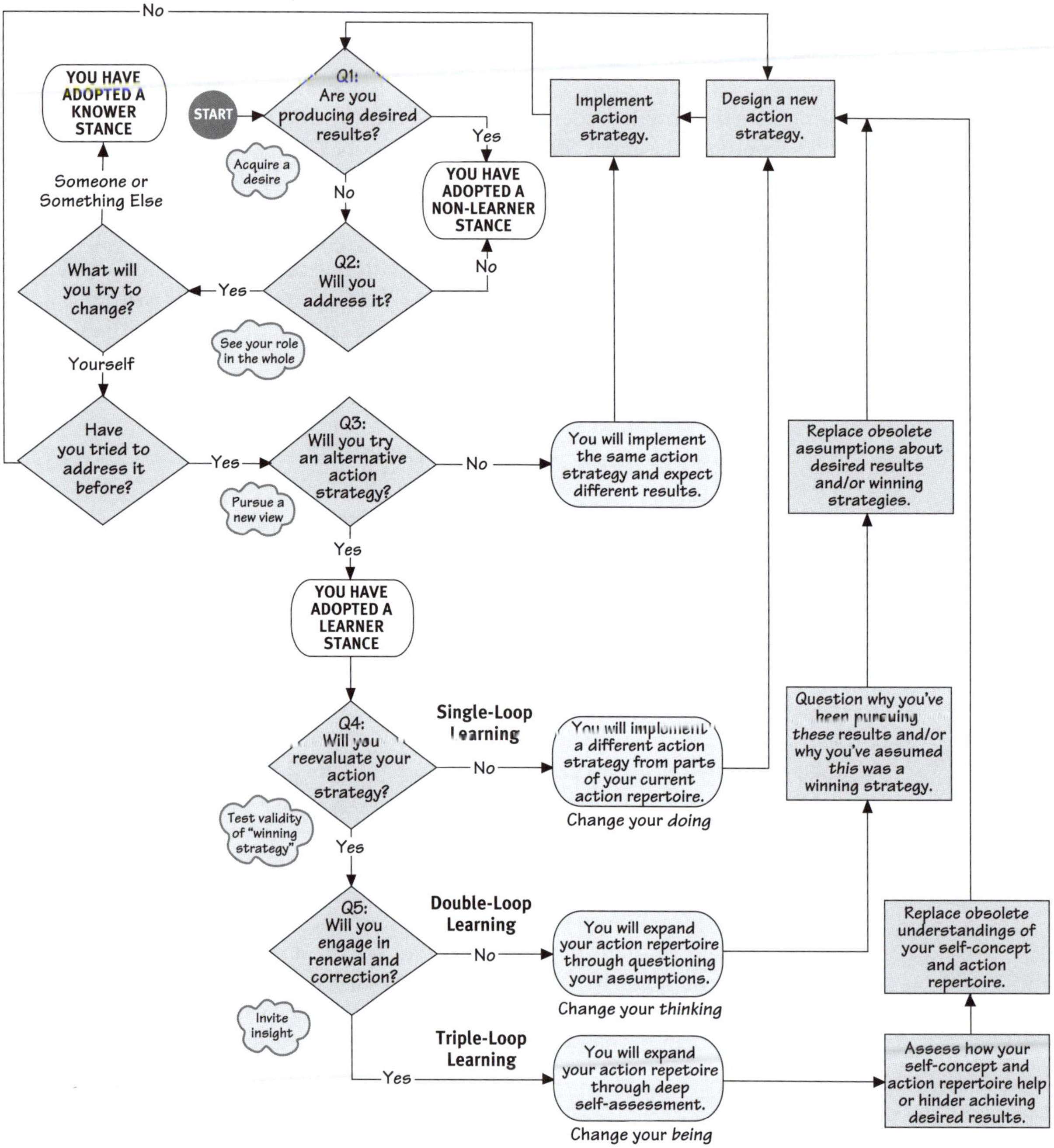

Figure 9-4

Simplified Learner's Path Decision Tree

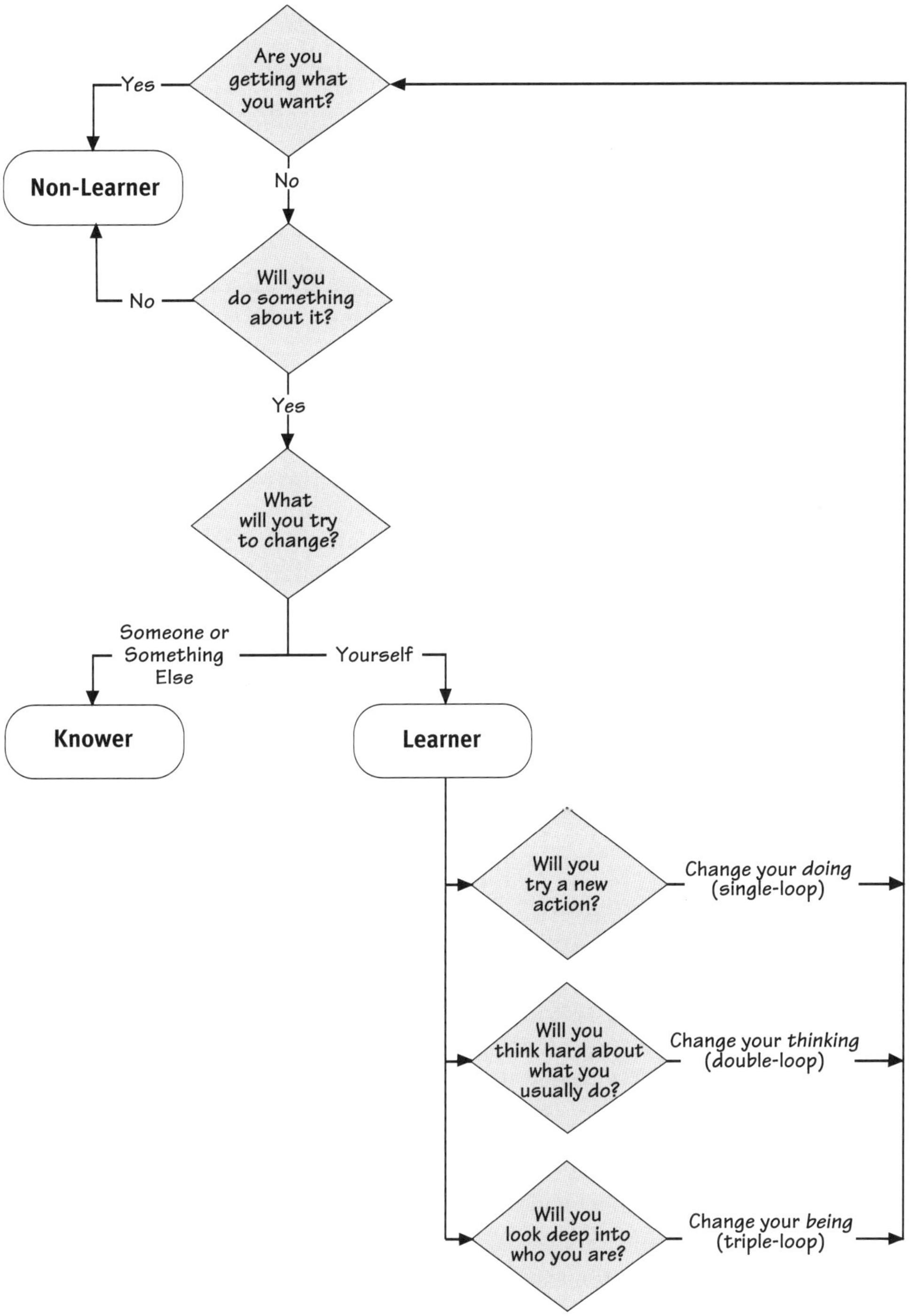

On the Path

This book is, in many ways, a chronicle of my own story of struggle, acknowledgment, and discovery about my knower addictions. Because of these admissions and struggles, I set out on a quest to find out how and why I came to be a knower. Along the way, I discovered a valuable path—the Learner's Path—and with it, became a *recovering knower*. May you, too, discover a path that leads you to achieve the results your heart desires.

Rapid Recap

- A self-guided map, showing the transformation from a learner to a deep learner, converts this chapter's advice into actionable advice.
- The Learner's Path Decision Tree is a convenient reference companion for responding to change through learning.

Reflective Response

- Identify an area in your life in which you have a deep desire to achieve a certain result but the action strategies you have been using, literally for years, have not enabled you to achieve it.

    - Which of the final two Learner's Path questions do you now face, and successfully answer, in order to make progress toward your desired result? Is it time to "use action strategies beyond your action repertoire" (test the validity of your winning strategies) or to "open up to renewal and correction" (invite insight)?

    - As a result of your experience with this book, how would you characterize yourself: a knower, a recovering knower, or a learner?

Afterword

Early this morning, I headed out in a boat, not long after sunrise, onto the lake at which I spent every summer as a boy. I had decided to go fishing. The wisps of fog swirl on the surface of the glassy water; the geese honk overhead; the air is cool and smells like morning; the sun has just started to peak over the treetops and illuminate the fog and warm my face. I've had poor luck fishing this morning, but I love the stillness of being out on the water, disturbed only by the occasional taunting of the fish as they leap and splash somewhere not far off.

I am in a reflective, melancholy mood. I'm reflecting on learning and thinking about this book. Last night, I started the final read-through of this manuscript before I must submit it as a final draft to the publisher. I'm wondering if I've done my best and if my best is good enough for this project to become a useful contribution to the field. Maybe what I'm feeling is not unlike what a parent feels just before sending their child away to college or down the aisle into marriage. Will they be okay out there in the world; have I done my best to prepare them to be successful?

My thoughtful tranquility is interrupted, however, when a speedboat rounds the bend and starts heading my way. It is pulling a couple of water-skiers; but not just any skiers—these guys are skiing barefoot. One guy I recognize as my former ski-mate. I stare with nostalgic interest (and some jealousy), remembering the times we skied together, years ago. Then suddenly, as if to rub my face in my lifelong inability to do the same, my friend, not more than 100 feet away, sits down, spins around to his back and rotates back up onto his feet—he executes a flawless tumbleturn. Now my emotions are having their way with me. All my youthful inadequacies come flooding back. How pathetic I must look to those unique, athletic, adventurers. I imagine they look at me, as I sit and cast my purple worm from our 23-year-old pontoon boat, and think to themselves, "Poor Brian, he just couldn't keep up with us. Look at him now. While we're out here footin', he sits drearily alone with a fishing pole in his hand. How sad."

How was I going to cope with these feelings of inadequacy? And beyond that, I was beginning to feel like a fraud. I remembered what I had written earlier in this book about how I applied double- and triple-loop learning to move *past* this inadequacy of not being able to do a tumbleturn. Now I was having a strong reaction in my area of vulnerability—like salt in a wound. How could I go forward in integrity with this book? Had I really learned as I said I did?

At that moment, I had to go deep into awareness and did some reflection: "Okay, what would a learner do? How am I going to respond effectively to these startling circumstances I now find myself in? If this learning stuff doesn't work *now*, I might as well just forget about this book." So I went into a dialogue with myself, and these thoughts passed through my head like lightning:

What is going on here?

I look like a fool here on this pontoon boat. I'd love to be out with them doing tumbleturns.

Why is that?

They can do tumbleturns and I can't. I feel like a failure. It's embarrassing to have them see me so passive.

Okay, let's use the Learner's Path to figure this out. First question: "Are you achieving desired results?"

No.

What do you want, then?

I want to do tumbleturns.

Alright, second question: "Will you address it—your inability to do tumbleturns?"

Actually . . . no. It would take a huge effort . . . and . . . I guess I really don't want it that bad.

Well then—you have nothing to learn then, do you? You're really not interested in learning to do a tumbleturn, are you?

No. I guess not.

What *are* you interested in accomplishing then? In what area are you not achieving desired results?

I want them to see me as something other than a "pontoon-boat fisherman." I used to be adventurous like them. Now look at me, sitting here passively! It's so unmanly.

So your desired result is to have them see you as a manly adventurer?

Yeah, I guess so.

Alright, second question again: "Will you address it?"

Yes, I will.

Okay, so on to the third question: "Will you try an alternative action strategy" in order to be seen as a manly adventurer?

Well, obviously doing tumbleturns hasn't worked. Come to think of it, golf hasn't worked either. Getting rich hasn't worked. I don't actually know what to do to have them see me as adventurous.

Alright. That's okay. Let's do some double-looping on that. Here's the fourth question: "Will you reevaluate your action repertoire?"

Yeah, I guess I better.

Why do you keep thinking that you have to compete to impress people?

Ooo, ouch. I don't know. I don't actually interact with those guys anymore anyway, so why do I care what they think of me? I'm going to have to let go of that (again). Competing with others is not the only way to have adventures and a productive and fulfilling life.

What *else* feels adventurous to you?

Well, actually, learning is an adventure—it's *always* an adventure, come to think of it.

Okay, great. Shall we go a little deeper—how about a little triple-looping? Here's the fifth question: "Will you engage in renewal and correction?"

Absolutely. I've got to get over this feeling of inadequacy for not doing a tumbleturn. Those guys out there—they are actually *learning*. They are learning to adapt the reduced strength and flexibility of their older bodies and still be able to ski and do tricks. It's amazing, really. I admire them for what they have been able to accomplish. They are having a great learning adventure. It's just my own sense of inadequacy that really provoked me to view them negatively. I put myself in this funk here.

That's good. You can see how you were getting in your own way. So, what kind of a learning adventure would *you* like to have . . . *right now?*

My thoughts wander back to fishing. I'm alone in this boat. My eight-year-old son is probably awake by now and waiting for me back at the cottage. Before we went to bed last night, we made a deal to go fishing together in the morning. I put my pole away, lift the anchors, set my face to the sun, and head back through the mist to pick him up and bring him out to learn the art of fishing. On the way, I pass a group of guys barefoot waterskiing. I admiringly, and without jealousy, wish them well.

Suddenly, it occurs to me. I have just passed through a fog of my inadequacies as a learner—in more ways than one. With renewed confidence and desire, I determine to build a legacy of learning with my son. A worthy, and adventurous, pursuit indeed.

Appendix 1
Bibliography

Anderson, Virginia, and Lauren Johnson. *Systems Thinking Basics: From Concepts to Causal Loops*. Pegasus Communications, 1997.

Argyris, Chris. *Overcoming Organizational Defenses*. Allyn & Bacon, 1990.

Argyris, Chris, Peter M. Senge, and Bill Noonan, "Managing Difficult Conversations (CD-ROM)," Harvard Business School Publishing, 2003.

Bandura, Albert. "Self-Efficacy," in *Encyclopedia of Human Behavior*. Edited by V. S. Ramachaudran. Vol. 4. Academic Press, 1994.

Block, Peter. "The Future of Workplace Learning and Performance," *Training and Development*, May 1994.

———. *Stewardship: Choosing Service over Self-Interest*. Berrett-Koehler, 1993.

Bolles, Richard Nelson. *How to Find Your Mission in Life*. Ten Speed Press, 2005.

———, *What Color Is Your Parachute? 2007: A Practical Manual for Job-Hunters and Career-Changers*. Ten Speed Press, 2006.

Covey, Stephen R. *The 7 Habits of Highly Effective People*. Fireside, 1989.

Covey, Stephen R., A. Roger Merrill, and Rebecca R. Merrill. *First Things First: To Live, to Love, to Learn, to Leave a Legacy*. Fireside, 1994.

Drucker, Peter. "How Schools Must Change," *Psychology Today*, May 1989.

Elrod II, P. David, and Donald D. Tippett. "The 'Death Valley' of Change," *Journal of Organizational Change Management* 15, No. 3 (2002): 273-291.

Fritz, Robert. *The Path of Least Resistance: Learning to Become the Creative Force in Your Own Life*. Ballantine, 1989.

Hargrove, Robert. *Masterful Coaching*. 2nd ed. Jossey-Bass/Pfeiffer, John Wiley & Sons, Inc., 2002.

Hoffer, Eric. *Reflections on the Human Condition*. Harper & Row, 1973.

Isaacs, William. *Dialogue: The Art of Thinking Together*. Currency/Doubleday, 1999.

Jones, Laurie Beth. *The Path: Creating Your Mission Statement for Work and for Life*. Hyperion, 1996.

Kofman, Fred. *Conscious Business: Transforming Your Workplace (and Yourself) by Changing the Way You Think, Act, and Communicate* (audiocassette). Sounds True, Inc., 2002.

———. *Conscious Business: How to Build Value Through Values* (compact disc and book). Sounds True, Inc., 2006.

———. "Learning, Knowledge and Power," Axialent, 2003. http://www.axialent.com.

Land, George and Beth Jarman. *Breakpoint and Beyond: Mastering the Future Today*. Harper's Business, 1992.

Senge, Peter. *The Fifth Discipline: The Art & Practice of the Learning Organization.* Currency/Doubleday, 1990.

———. *Senge on Change and Learning,* Pegasus Communication, 2003.

Senge, Peter, Art Kleiner, Charlotte Roberts, Richard Ross, and Bryan Smith. *The Fifth Discipline Fieldbook: Strategies and Tools for Building a Learning Organization*. Currency/Doubleday, 1994.

Stone, Douglas, Bruce Patton, Sheila Heen, and Roger Fisher. *Difficult Conversations: How to Discuss What Matters Most*. Viking, 1999.

Vaill, Peter. *Learning As a Way of Being: Strategies for Survival in a World of Permanent White Water*. Jossey-Bass/Pfeiffer, John Wiley & Sons, Inc., 1996.

Woodward, Harry. *Navigating Through Change*. McGraw-Hill, 1994.

Yankelovich, Daniel. *The Magic of Dialogue: Transforming Conflict into Cooperation*. Touchstone/Simon & Schuster, Inc., 1999.

Appendix 2
Glossary of Terms

[Note: words in *italics* are defined elsewhere in the glossary]

Action Repertoire. The stock of *action strategies* a person has reliably used in the past to achieve *desired results.*

Action Strategy. An intended course of action for achieving a *desired result.*

Actual Result. The outcome or effect of some action or situation, whether intended or not.

Awakener. Internally or externally generated information that causes a person to acknowledge a discrepancy between his or her *desired* and *actual results.*

Awareness. A conscious sense of recognition of something within or outside of oneself; mindfulness; attentively perceiving and experiencing one's inner and outer reality; not relying on instincts and habits.

Desired Result. The intended outcome or effect of some action or situation.

Double-Loop Learning. Achieving *desired results* by changing one's "thinking": questioning one's prevailing mental framework, and replacing obsolete assumptions about *desired results* and/or *winning strategies.*

Knower. A person who actively hides his or her lack of *knowledge* from others, and is unwilling to be influenced.

Knowledge. The ability to produce *desired results.*

Learner. A person who actively increases his or her ability to produce *desired results.*

Learning. Increasing one's ability to produce *desired results.*

Learning Culture/Organization. A community of *learners* and *recovering knowers* in an organization that values and promotes *learning.*

Learning Disciplines. A collection of tools, methods, and practices that, when consistently practiced, facilitate becoming a *learner* and then living as a *learner*. Five primary learning disciplines, as defined by Peter Senge in *The Fifth Discipline*, include: *personal mastery, shared vision, systems thinking, mental models,* and *team learning*.

Mental Models. A learning discipline for reflecting on one's attitudes and perceptions, thereby increasing mutual understanding and insight into oneself.

Non-Learner. A person who is unaware of, uninterested in, or ambivalent about any possible discrepancy between his or her *desired* and *actual results*.

Personal Mastery. A learning discipline for developing personal effectiveness and the ability to create the results one most desires.

Recovering Knower. A person who actively attempts to overcome his or her dependence on the *secrets of a knower* by practicing the *learning disciplines*.

Secrets of a Knower. A set of thinking habits that simultaneously protect a person from the threat or embarrassment of "not knowing" and prevent him or her from making progress along *The Learner's Path*.

Self-Concept. The mental image a person has of him or her self and his or her strengths, weaknesses, status, qualities, personal worth, etc.

Shared Vision. A learning discipline for creating collective aspiration and mutual commitment.

Single-Loop Learning. Achieving *desired results* by changing one's "doing": taking new actions within the prevailing mental framework one is operating under.

Systems Thinking. A learning discipline for understanding the whole, and how structures and systems are interconnected.

Team Learning. A learning discipline for generating collective insight by transforming how a group thinks and interacts.

The Learner's Path. A conceptual framework that describes the underlying process of *learning*.

Triple-Loop Learning. Achieving *desired results* by changing one's "being": engaging in deep self-assessment, and replacing obsolete understandings of one's *self-concept* and *action repertoire*.

Winning Strategy. An *action strategy* that a person relies on, uses frequently, and considers to be his or her strength, when, in reality, it can have a limiting effect on achieving one's true *desired results*. At best, winning strategies can produce the usual results.

Appendix 3
Additional Resources

The titles below are available through www.pegasuscom.com.

Newsletters

The Systems Thinker®

Leverage Points for a New Workplace, New World®

Workbooks

Systems Thinking Basics: From Concepts to Causal Loops, Virginia Anderson and Lauren Johnson

Systems Archetypes Basics: From Story to Structure, Daniel H. Kim and Virginia Anderson

Books

The Fifth Discipline: The Art & Practice of the Learning Organization, Peter M. Senge

The Fifth Discipline Fieldbook, Peter M. Senge et al.

The Dance of Change: The Challenges of Sustaining Momentum in Learning Organizations, Peter M. Senge et al.

Schools That Learn: A Fifth Discipline Fieldbook for Educators, Parents, and Everyone Who Cares About Education, Peter M. Senge et al.

Presence: An Exploration of Profound Change in People, Society, and Organizations, Peter M. Senge, et al.

Outlearning the Wolves: Surviving and Thriving in a Learning Organization, David Hutchens

Shadows of the Neanderthal: Illuminating the Beliefs That Limit Our Organizations, David Hutchens

The Lemming Dilemma: Living with Purpose, Leading with Vision, David Hutchens

The Tip of the Iceberg: Managing the Hidden Forces That Can Make or Break Your Organization, David Hutchens

Listening to the Volcano: Conversations That Open Our Minds to New Possibilities, David Hutchens

Short Volumes

Dialogue at Work: Skills for Leveraging Collective Understanding, Glenna Gerard and Linda Ellinor

The Essentials of Servant-Leadership: Principles in Practice, Ann McGee-Cooper and Gary Looper

Introduction to Systems Thinking, Daniel H. Kim

Laminated Pocket Guides

The Ladder of Inference

Private Conversation: The Left-Hand Column

Productive Conversations: Using Advocacy and Inquiry Effectively

A Guide to Practicing Dialogue

Guidelines for Daily Systems Thinking Practice

Eye of the Needle: A Communication Tool

Vision Deployment Matrix I: Shifting from a Reactive to a Generative Orientation

Vision Deployment Matrix II: Crossing the Chasm from Reality to Vision

Audio and Video Recordings

One on One: Senge on Leadership, Peter M. Senge

One on One: Senge on Change and Learning, Peter M. Senge

Enhancing Collaboration by Challenging Our Mental Models, Marc-André Olivier

Introduction to Systems Thinking: An Overview, Ginny Wiley

The Potential of Talking and the Challenge of Listening, Adam Kahane

Systems Thinking for Collaboration: The Role of Mental Models, David Peter Stroh and Michael Goodman

PEGASUS COMMUNICATIONS, INC. helps individuals, teams, and organizations thrive in an increasingly complex world. Since 1989, innovators working to spark and sustain positive change in the systems they care about have looked to Pegasus for resources and networking opportunities. Through a grounding in the rigorous principles and tools of systems thinking and related disciplines, practitioners from business, education, government, and the nonprofit world find the freedom to connect with others in new ways and design sustainable solutions to their most persistent challenges. From tentative first steps to great leaps of faith, we provide tools and ideas for changing the world one system at a time.

PEGASUS COMMUNICATIONS, INC.
One Moody Street
Waltham, MA 02453-5339

Phone: (781) 398-9700
Fax: (781) 894-7175
Web Site: www.pegasuscom.com